Gilles Deleuze

PARALLAX   RE-VISIONS OF CULTURE
             AND SOCIETY

Stephen G. Nichols, Gerald Prince, and Wendy Steiner
SERIES EDITORS

Gilles Deleuze

Cinema and Philosophy

Paola Marrati

Translated by Alisa Hartz

The Johns Hopkins University Press
Baltimore

This book has been brought to publication with the generous assistance of the Humanities Center and the Krieger School of Arts and Sciences at the Johns Hopkins University.

Originally published as *Gilles Deleuze: Cinéma et philosophie,* © 2003 Presses Universitaires de France

Johns Hopkins Paperback edition, 2012
9 8 7 6 5 4 3 2 1

The Johns Hopkins University Press
2715 North Charles Street
Baltimore, Maryland 21218-4363
www.press.jhu.edu

The Library of Congress has cataloged the hardcover edition of this book as follows:

Marrati, Paola.
    Gilles Deleuze : cinema and philosophy / Paola Marrati ; translated by Alisa Hartz.
        p. cm. — (Parallax, re-visions of culture and society)
    Includes bibliographical references and index.
    ISBN-13: 978-0-8018-8802-1 (hardcover : alk. paper)
    ISBN-10: 0-8018-8802-6 (hardcover : alk. paper)
    1. Motion pictures—Philosophy. 2. Deleuze, Gilles, 1925–1995. I. Title.
    PN1995.M296 2008
    791.4301—dc22   2007035483

A catalog record for this book is available from the British Library.

ISBN-13: 978-1-4214-0791-3
ISBN-10: 1-4214-0791-4

Special discounts are available for bulk purchases of this book. For more information, please contact Special Sales at 410-516-6936 or specialsales@press.jhu.edu.

To Léo and Hent

Contents

.

Preface to the English-language Edition

Deleuze's two books on cinema, *Cinema 1: The Movement-Image* and *Cinema 2: The Time-Image,* even more than his other works, call for different audiences and different readings. They obviously are of interest to students and scholars of film and media, as well as to philosophers and critical theorists engaged with Deleuze's thinking. But they also get attention across disciplinary boundaries. *Cinema 1* and *2* offer challenging analyses of modes of perception. They describe a plurality of equally compelling ways of linking past, present, and future, ways that may exclude each other, but that, more often than not, overlap and coexist, giving to time, and to our experience of it, a thick, layered fabric. Together these books provide innovative concepts to help us think about the power of images, affects, and beliefs, about the power of the mind and of the body—all of which we know, in fact, so little about. It does not come as a surprise, then, that both books increasingly find readers in all the fields of the humanities and social sciences. No one can say whether "the century will be Deleuzian," as Foucault—somehow ironically—predicted, but the reception of Deleuze's work in general, and on cinema in particular, is in this regard only at its beginning.

Cinema 1 and *2* are difficult books, however, and their cross-disciplinary appeal makes it all the more important that their dense philosophical arguments and underpinnings should be closely analyzed and unpacked. I hope that this study contributes to such a task and that it will prove helpful to all readers of Deleuze.

My aim in this preface is not to map out the recent reception of Deleuze's work on cinema across disciplines. Such a reception is still in the making, and, to my mind, it is too early to attempt a general overview of its influence. Further, such an enterprise, no matter how important and useful it might be, belongs to the field of intellectual history and is therefore a task I am not prepared to undertake. Nor is this preface meant to be a description of the content of the book; the introduction fulfills that necessary function. My aim is rather to advance a claim that, as such, is not explicitly made in the book for the compelling reason that it was not one of the guiding hypotheses of my study but, rather, imposed itself upon me while I was writing, as a consequence of the analyses undertaken.

The claim is this: *Cinema 1* and *2* are the key texts in which Deleuze develops his *political philosophy*. This is not to deny the importance of the more openly political books such as *Anti-Oedipus* or *A Thousand Plateaus,* nor is it to deny the significance of Deleuze's collaboration with Félix Guattari. It is even less to argue that cinema is not the real object of the books but only a pretext to write about politics. As I hope to show, Deleuze takes absolutely seriously the Bergsonian injunction that philosophy needs precision and has to elaborate singular concepts that fit singular objects, and them alone, if it wants to avoid building general systems of explanation that can be, indeed, applied to everything but only because of their emptiness. My hypothesis is a different one: it is that precisely because Deleuze aims to grasp the specificity of cinema, its novelty, as well as the novelty of its different instances, that he is led to analyze in detail *forms of action and agency* and their transformations. It is such a close analysis of agency that constitutes, to my mind, the political contribution of *Cinema 1* and *2*.

While the regime of movement-images, as Deleuze understands it, is not reducible to the action-image form, it is undeniable that *Cinema 1* dwells extensively on films that make of the action-image their organizing center. Affection-images and perception-images are always present, but they rarely constitute the organizing principle of a film. This is why classic cinema mostly privileges the action form and the active montage—be it organic, as in Griffith, or dialectic, as in Eisenstein. The rise of modern cinema in the aftermath of World War II, in Deleuze's analyses, marks the demise of the action form in favor of different forms of montage that undo the primacy of action and present other links among perceptions, affections, and agency. Such a modern cinema is the explicit object of *Cinema 2,* which explores the upsurge of films that no longer subordinate time to movement or action but rather aim at making time, as such, perceptible.

If this is the most recognizable, and recognized, move of the books, some of its implications have not been sufficiently spelled out—namely what the analyses of the action-image form has to say about both liberal and Marxist-inspired political theories and what the analysis of the time-image regimes have to say about the political consequences of the primacy of "time" over "movement." I would like to argue that the action form, as Deleuze describes it, corresponds to liberal and historicist notions of subjectivity and agency, while the rise of time-images, in the sense Deleuze gives to the term, should not be understood as the simple, and easy, claim that there is no future for (political) action but, on the contrary, as an effort to think agency anew, along different lines than those prescribed by liberalism and historicism. Such a Deleuzian approach to agency is grounded on an understanding of modernity that, for not being mainstream, deserves attention if one wants to fully grasp it.

The insistence with which Deleuze highlights the similarity between Griffith's and Eisenstein's concept and practice of montage is significant in this regard. Certainly, Eisenstein has a very different notion of the laws that govern the life of a human society than Griffith has, but they both understand it as an organic unity whose elements are held together by necessary, and coherent, ties. Eisenstein's criticism of Griffith's "bourgeois" form of montage is grounded precisely on such a shared assumption. Griffith does not grasp the dialectic nature of the laws that govern the life of the social organism, its growth, tensions, and crises; he wrongly assumes that the elements of the organism are naturally given instead of being historically produced, and he fails to see that what threatens its unity or recomposes it at a higher level is not of the order of individual passions, desires, or betrayals. In both cases, however, what sets in motion the life of the organism are actions. What gives significance to affects, ideas, desires, and values is the realm of possible actions. As Bergson writes: "perception is master of space in the exact measure in which action is master of time."[1]

Time itself, personal or historical, becomes significant only as the frame in which actions unfold. The definition of time as "measure of movement" goes back to Aristotle, but if Deleuze repeatedly recalls it in his *Cinema* books, it is because it also applies to more recent notions of subjectivity and history structured around the primacy of action. Such a primacy curves the universe, as Bergson writes, giving to it an organizing center, and in doing so, action shapes *both space and time*. Time takes on the form of the linear sequence of the past, present, and future of the action: it measures the movements of an acting subject.

For Deleuze, such a logic of action presents a powerful and consistent way of understanding the bonds that humans create between them, their social and natural milieu, their individual and collective history. Such a logic of action is, for Deleuze, what sustains a specific form of subjectivity, as well as dominant conceptions of politics. Liberal theories of democracy—be they Rawlsian or Habermasian—rely on, explicitly or implicitly, the notion of an individual subject whose rationality is primarily understood as a capacity for action. But political theories, Marxist or otherwise oriented, that focus on a collective subjectivity also define it mainly in terms of action. The individual or historical political subject is the subject of action (in the sense Deleuze gives to the term). The action-image is a cinematographic device, but it spells out the continuity of individual and collective ways of understanding social and historical life as oriented *by* and *toward* action. I would further argue that recent theories of sovereignty do not question the primacy of action but only displace its actor: the decisive action is no longer carried out by an individual or collective subject but by an almighty and unfathomable "sovereign power."

As is well known, classic cinema, for Deleuze, lost for us its power of conviction long ago, and, arguably, the same holds true of political projects grounded on the primacy of action and the specific temporality it expresses. But can politics forgo action? Can we even think of politics, at least progressive politics, no longer shaped by human agency and oriented toward a (better) future? Deleuze's analyses of modern cinema dwell extensively on the complex, layered nature of time, on the different forms of time-images; he remains silent, though, on new possibilities of agency, as if we would have to forgo action, as if we could forgo action. His famous descriptions of Italian neorealism as a cinema of the seer, where the characters are no longer able to act in response to the situation and are more spectators than agents, would seem to confirm the idea that, for Deleuze, not only a specific form of agency is lost for us but agency itself.

This reading, however, misses a crucial point of Deleuze's analyses. It is not out of passivity, powerlessness, or resignation that one is no longer capable of immediately and "appropriately" responding to a given situation or event. It is quite the opposite: the response is suspended because one has become aware that *certain actions* are *powerless*. Habits of conduct, patterns of behavior, are deemed to express weakness or strength, love or contempt, indignation or revolt. Not to engage in the appropriate response, not to express the appropriate affect may seem to imply passivity, or worse. Deleuze's point, though, is that sometimes, perhaps even often, "acting in the appropriate way" *is* precisely the lack of response and the *refusal* to acknowledge our helplessness. The display of military power may not be the solution to new, or old, dangers, but it certainly conveys, for a time, the illusion of being in control, of knowing what the situation is about and knowing what to do about it. Following the logic of Deleuze's argument, one could say that these actions are likely to be acts of denial, hiding in "need for action" both the inability to truly respond to the challenge and the awareness of inadequacy.

Deleuze insisted on the importance of learning *to perceive in order to perceive* and not just to react, on the power of contemplation, and the need for time and thought is perfectly pertinent for politics. Deleuze describes modern cinema as a cinema in search of more thought. This is not to say that classic cinema was stupid; it is to say, rather, that new situations require new cinematic forms because the old ones have lost their power of conviction for us. The same holds true for politics: politics need more thought (and creativity) instead of empty mimicries of the past. Along the same lines, certainly there is no politics without agency, but agency requires more than the fiction of a self-transparent and almighty subject.

Deleuze's claim that modern cinema sets time free from its subordination to movement does not say that movements and actions are frozen in a still time; it does not say that films become "slow" (even if some may). It says that movements and actions no longer shape both time and space but rather that they occur in time and space, which is a very different statement. The line of the universe is no longer described by, or centered on, our possible actions; actions—along with affects, perceptions, and thoughts—take place, respond, or fail to respond, to each other, react to each other, or not. In short: not only "actions" have agency, and the agency they do have does not go straight from one action to another one. In Deleuze's view, we certainly need more thought to follow the tracks of multiple agencies; we certainly need more thought to create "new forms of life"; but we also need, maybe in the first place, to acknowledge the power of thought. Such an insistence on the importance of thinking may seem trivial, especially coming from a philosopher. And it would be so if Deleuze, following Heidegger, did not constantly remind us how difficult it is to think, and that in fact, most of the time, we *do not* think.[2]

Certainly, Deleuze's analyses of modern cinema do not produce a new model of agency endowed with the consistency and simplicity of the organic and/or dialectic form of the action-image. It may be difficult to renounce the image's power and the belief in the redemptive (and transcendent) function of the future that underlies it, but the fact is there is nothing we have to renounce: we no longer believe in organic ties or dialectical laws. We can act "as if" we still believe in those ties or laws to avoid the complexities of the present; we can deny that they no longer carry any power of conviction for us, but these are only reactive moves. And it is reactive, although in a different way, to turn back, in a nostalgic mood, toward a (mythical) better past. The critical task of thinking, for Deleuze, must avoid both nostalgia and denial in order to be creative. Cinema appeared to Deleuze to be highly innovative in all regards (bad films notwithstanding), and modern cinema was particularly capable of exploring new forms of agency folded in time, linked in more complex ways to perceptions, affects, and thoughts. It had lost a certain "realism" and the simplicity of the classic form, but in doing so, it gained deeper layers of reality and subjectivity. In this regard, one may say that cinema, for Deleuze, was in advance of philosophy and politics, which, most of the time, overplay the sovereignty of the action. And it explains, I believe, why the best political philosophy of Gilles Deleuze can be found in his *Cinema* books.

▌ *Acknowledgments*

I am deeply indebted to those who heightened my interest in Deleuze: Denis Guénoun, because of our conversations, and Ghislaine Glasson-Deschaumes, because she invited me to talk about minorities to a complex audience at a difficult time—graduate students from all the Balkan countries during the war: I found myself at a loss, and I started reading *A Thousand Plateaus* on the concept of becoming "minoritarian." Thanks to that occasion I found a way of engaging with a philosopher who had been utterly alien to me for a long time.

I am equally indebted to those with whom I have watched so many movies: Hent de Vries, my daughter Léo, and several other friends. Thanks to their company, I have come to discover, and often enjoy, films and genres to which I would not spontaneously have been drawn. I believe now that being exposed to a wide range of styles and registers—from contemporary Asian cinema to Harry Potter, for instance—constitutes my most precious cinematographic education. Although these experiences and the thoughts they have provoked are not explicitly present in this study, they were constantly on my mind when I was writing it and, I am convinced, play an important role in the analyses the book develops.

The book is also, according to a different temporality, deeply indebted to those with whom I have been—and hope to continue to be—in conversation in more recent years. Friends, colleagues, and students. I name them here, *faute de mieux,* in alphabetical order: Jane Bennett, Jay Bernstein, Judith Butler, William Connolly, Veena Das, Aaron Goodfellow, Denis Guénoun, Alex Lefebvre, Todd Meyers, Eric Michaud, Alessia Ricciardi, Matthew Scherer, Nils Schott,

Acknowledgments

Hent de Vries. And to Léo, who continues to teach me so much. I would also like to thank my colleagues at the Humanities Center and other departments at the Johns Hopkins University: it is difficult to imagine a more challenging and congenial intellectual context. All these conversations are precious, and inspiring, to my intellectual and emotional life.

A special acknowledgment goes to François Zourabichvili, who decided to end his life in the spring of 2006. I cannot judge his act; nobody can: I only want to say how much I miss him, as a philosopher—one of the rare who rigorously read Deleuze—and as a friend.

Frequently Cited Texts

Frequently cited texts appear in parentheses and are referenced by the following abbreviations. For full bibliographical references, see Works Cited. Page numbers separated with a virgule refer first to the English translation and then to the original.

By Gilles Deleuze
C1   *Cinema 1: The Movement-Image*
C2   *Cinema 2: The Time-Image*

By Gilles Deleuze and Félix Guattari
WPh *What Is Philosophy?*

By Henri Bergson
CE   *Creative Evolution*
MM *Matter and Memory*

Gilles Deleuze

▌ *Introduction*

This work aims to give an analytic presentation of the two books that Gilles Deleuze devoted to cinema, *Cinema 1: The Movement-Image* and *Cinema 2: The Time-Image,* on three axes: (1) the innovative contribution of Deleuze's analyses to the field of cinema theory, (2) the philosophical issues of broader significance, and (3) the place of *Cinema 1* and *2* in Deleuze's oeuvre as a whole. These three aspects are inseparable and must be studied conjointly in order for us to understand the multiple stakes of Deleuze's philosophy of cinema.

Deleuze and Theories of Cinema

Cinema 1 and *2* make a very important contribution to the field of cinema theory. Deleuze's work goes against the grain of two trends that dominated cinematographical studies in France, and spread to other countries, from the postwar period to the 1980s: the realist and phenomenological approach of André Bazin, on the one hand, and the linguistic and psychoanalytical approach of Christian Metz, on the other. Deleuze's distance from the two is not, however, symmetrical; even as he rejects Bazin's realism, Deleuze is profoundly marked by the theme of a cinema of time, which he adopts and develops in an original manner. Phenomenologically oriented approaches cannot account for what belongs to cinema itself insofar as they retain subjective or "natural" perception as the model of reference, whereas the specificity of cinematographic perception lies precisely in the fact that it cannot be referred back to any subjective center. Cinema's specificity is also underestimated by linguistic approaches, which assimilate images to utterances. Deleuze's project is thus to extract an "essence" of cinema, to describe what belongs exclusively to cinema, and to analyze how and in what singular modes cinema thinks in images themselves. To describe the specificity of cinema, Deleuze offers a classification of different types of filmic images that, without claiming to be exhaustive, nonetheless takes into account the whole history of cinema such as it unfolded before the advent of digital images. This classification turns on two key concepts: the *movement-image* and the *time-image.* The elaboration of the concepts of movement-image and time-image (and their different types) allows Deleuze to produce a properly cinematographic semiology of great richness and to reorganize the major debates that run through the history of cinema around a general problematic. The concept of the movement-image gives him a new perspective from which to consider debates on the relation between montage and shot and between cinema and narration. The concept of the time-image allows him to account for the mutation that occurred in postwar cinema and for the break that separated "classic" cinema from "modern" cinema. The articulation between movement-image and time-image marks not only an *internal* articulation in the history of cinema but also an articulation between cinema, the other arts, and a certain state of the world. From Deleuze's classification of images emerges a history of cinema as history of the aesthetic, political, and philosophical issues of the twentieth century.

Philosophical Stakes

The concepts of movement-image and time-image are strictly philosophical concepts; we must therefore analyze what cinema gives philosophy to think. A central issue is the status of representation. Far from confirming Heidegger's famous theses on modernity as the age of representation, cinema radically calls them into question. Because of a false appearance, we are led to believe that cinema, a technical "art," falls within the frame of the double movement in which man becomes a subject at the same time that the world itself becomes image. Yet cinema does not summon an image-world before the gaze of a spectator-subject. Rather, cinema's particularity is to produce images that are irreducible to the model of subjective perception. It is in relation to this general context that one must understand Deleuze's analyses of the status of cinematographic perception, his rejection of realist and phenomenological approaches that, directly or indirectly, presuppose a theory of representation, as well as the fundamental importance he grants to the first chapter of Bergson's *Matter and Memory*. The universe described by Bergson is ruled by a strict equivalence between images, matter, light, and movement. These movement-images—Deleuze's term—form a radically acentered universe in which perception does not wait for the human gaze to emerge. Because of the equivalence between movement and light, images in themselves are perception, perception of matter that needs no consciousness in order to become visible. Conscious perception surges as a special image, a "living image" that, rather than reacting to all the movements of other images, is able to make a selection among them. This selection is dictated by the interests and needs of life: perception becomes conscious on the condition that it perceive less, retaining only the useful aspects of things. These are the two major points where Bergson distances himself from a long philosophical tradition: light is not "in" consciousness but in things themselves, and, from the outset, conscious perception is linked to action rather than disinterested contemplation. These are also the two aspects that allow Deleuze to join Bergson's philosophy with cinema. On the one hand, because of montage and the mobile camera, cinema can show an acentered universe of movement-images in which subjective perceptions do, of course, emerge but in which they have no privilege whatsoever but are merely singular movements among the movements of the world. Moreover, if most great films of classic cinema (American films, but also Soviet and European) are structured around the link between perception and action (what Deleuze calls the "action form"), cinema has always been able to undo this link. It was able to produce images that go beneath subjective perception and tend to rejoin the perception of matter itself, just as it created images in which perception is no longer directly connected to action but creates new links with images that come from time and thought. According to Deleuze, this is where the distinction is played out between classic cinema and modern, postwar cinema, first with Italian neorealism and then with the French New Wave. This cinema, where what is at stake is no longer "see[ing] in order to act" but "see[ing] in order to see," as Bergson's *Creative Evolution* puts it, is still Bergsonian in its exploration of dimensions of a nonchronological time that Bergson, for his part, had also pursued.

Cinema 1 *and* 2 *in Deleuze's Oeuvre*

If cinema is Bergsonian, as Deleuze writes, it also led Deleuze to read Bergson in a different way. Bergson was always important to Deleuze's oeuvre, but Bergson was nonetheless somehow absent in relation to a central issue in Deleuze's philosophy: immanence, or more precisely, the definition of the plane of immanence. Now, the analysis of *Matter and Memory*'s universe of movement-images, an essential piece of the project of a philosophy of cinema, is undertaken using these very concepts. This has many consequences, and one of the tasks of *What Is Philosophy?* is to make them explicit. Deleuze does not rescind his critique of what he called, as early as *Nietzsche and Philosophy*, the "dogmatic image of thought," that is to say, a set of implicit presuppositions that mislead us as to the nature of thought. But the encounter with cinema led Deleuze to reconsider the ontological status of images. Images are capable of all sorts of movement and are affected by all dimensions of time. Therefore they participate fully in the plane of immanence. *What Is Philosophy?* takes fully into account what had been established in *Cinema 1* and *2*. There, a multiplicity of immanent images of thought are substituted for the singular and dogmatic one, and, for the first time, the Bergson of the first chapter of *Matter and Memory* takes his place alongside Spinoza in the line of philosophers of immanence. This is not the only major shift following the books on cinema. The project of describing the singular essence of cinema raises another explicit question that will be central to *What Is Philosophy?,* that of the singularity of philosophy itself, of what brings art, philosophy, and science—forms of thought and creation—together and yet maintains their distinctions. Finally, the analysis of the crisis of the action form in cinema led Deleuze to frame more broadly the problem of the broken link between humans and the world. The revolutionary dreams of early American and European cinema did not fulfill their promises. But in its great moments, cinema never stopped filming the faith in new modes of existence still to be discovered. Through cinema, a face of modernity emerges: the face not of the death of God but of the loss of the world. What we lack is an immanent belief in this world: not a belief in its existence, which no one doubts, but in the possibility of creating new forms of life in it. *What Is Philosophy?* devotes extensive analyses to the modern problem of an immanent conversion of faith. The strictly philosophical legacy of *Cinema 1* and *2* is thus extremely significant.

1 Images in Movement and Movement-Images

Draw out of the movement the mobility which is its essence.

Henri Bergson, *Matter and Memory*

There is no doubt that cinema was one of the twentieth century's great inventions. It was art, but it also accompanied whole generations as they went about their daily lives. It was *modern* art, if only because it managed, like no other art of the twentieth century, to be part of all our lives. This is precisely what Deleuze acknowledges in the last lines of the preface to the French edition of *Cinema 1,* where he justifies the absence of reproductions in the book by calling on "the great films, of which each of us retains to a greater or lesser extent a memory, emotion, or perception" (xiv/8). Stanley Cavell, too, invokes this collective memory in his books on cinema. The situation may have altered some time ago, but the fact remains that cinema has been able to inscribe its history within our collective memory, and we have yet to assess the significance of such a fact.[1]

But what is new about cinema? What makes cinema an essential feature of the twentieth century? Or in other words, where do films, the great films and the lesser, draw that power of emotion and perception that has left so many traces in our memory? *Cinema 1* and *2* provide Deleuze's answers to these questions and to many others. Before addressing their broader significance, we must analyze the first distinctive characteristic of cinema: *movement.* For the novelty brought about by cinema is first and foremost movement in images. Where other visual arts—from mask making to painting, from sculpture to photography—produce static images, which, even when they are images of movement, must be frozen in a certain pose, cinema sets images themselves in movement. We must therefore look to movement for cinema's difference, or for its own nature.

But what kind of movement is concerned? If, as Deleuze believes, we need to think the essence of cinema, that which belongs to cinema and to cinema alone, the first precaution we must take is to avoid using concepts that are too broad or too abstract. For that matter, this precaution concerns not only cinema but philosophy as the exercise of thought. Very early in his work, Deleuze adopted Bergson's demand for "precision in philosophy": philosophy must fit tightly to its object.[2] Most philosophical systems produce concepts so abstract (movement, time, being, the one, the multiple, etc.) that they can be applied to anything and everything: to reality, to the possible, and even to the impossible. The explanatory power of such concepts is only superficial: they can account for everything insofar as they are concerned with nothing in particular. But there should be no space between a philosophical concept and its object: precision requires concepts that are "tailor-made." Precise concepts delimit singular objects and these objects alone. There should be no gap between experience and its explanation, even when the aim is to understand the conditions of experience and to return to its sources. If one thereby goes beyond experience—and we will see that this is necessary—it is not in order to reach the "conditions of every possible experience," as in Kant, but to reach the conditions of real experience.[3] *Cinema 1* and *2* are written under the auspices of this requirement: their aim is to produce the singular concepts that belong to cinema. This endeavor leads Deleuze to deepen this theme, always present in his work, and to reformulate it in a new direction. But before analyzing the way Deleuze's books on cinema shifted his philosophical itinerary, their stakes must be unfolded.

It is therefore not enough to say that cinema introduces movement in images; the kind of movement proper to cinematographic images must be specified. The first chapter of *Cinema 1*, "Theses on movement: First commentary on Bergson," introduces a series of distinctions and extracts different aspects of movement. According to Deleuze, it is important to determine precisely the technological conditions of cinema: defining it as a projection system that refers to a photographic framework is not sufficient. Cinema depends not on the photo in general but on the snapshot, the equidistance of snapshots, and their transfer to a framework that constitutes the "film." Long-exposure photos and older image-projection systems such as shadow puppets are not part of the same technological lineage as cinema because cinema is a system that reproduces not "movement in general" but movement "as a function of any-instant-whatever, that is, as a function of equidistant instants, selected so as to create an impression of continuity" (*C1*, 5/14). Cinema decomposes and recomposes movement in relation to equidistant any-instant-whatevers: it produces a sensible and immanent analysis of movement, meaning that movement is described in a continuity rather than being an inevitable but ultimately inessential transition between two figures, two shots, or two poses. Certain forms of dance and mime are punctuated by climaxes, by poses or forms that are finally attained: they do of course bring movement into play, but the movement in question is only the passage between one pose and another and holds no interest in itself.[4] These systems imply not an analysis but a synthesis of movement and, indeed, an ideal (or transcendent) synthesis insofar as movement is merely the transition between forms that alone have value and are supposed to precede movement.

Viewed from this perspective, cinema is the last descendant of the transformation produced by the modern scientific revolution. Kepler's astronomy, Galileo's physics, or Cartesian geometry were in fact based on an analytical conception of movement; they considered movement at any moment whatever and rejected the idea of privileged instants. It is for this very reason, Deleuze remarks, that cinema in its early days was greeted with more skepticism than enthusiasm. Cinema seemed to hold little interest because it was based on a scientific conception of movement that had been accepted for centuries and because its artistic interest was equally dubious insofar as art seemed to be consecrated to a nobler kind of movement, that of the synthesis of forms. Such was the ambiguity of cinema's beginnings: an "industrial art," it was "neither an art nor a science" (*C1*, 6/16).

This analytic character of cinematographic movement attracted Henri Bergson's attention as early as 1907 in *Creative Evolution*. In order to reproduce any movement whatever on screen—the movement, for example, of a regiment marching by—cinema proceeds first of all through decomposition. First, a series of snapshots is taken, with the march appearing in an immobile position in each. Next, these snapshots are juxtaposed and projected on a screen. A series of immobile images of successive positions is then animated, but it is animated through an entirely exterior movement. As it unrolls through the camera, the strip of film bestows the illusion of movement on images that are in themselves static. In this sense, according to Bergson, cinema's operation is doubly artificial: rather than catching movements as they are happening, it must do with immobile shots from which, with the help of the camera, it then extracts an impersonal and abstract movement, "movement in general" (*CE*, 304/304). But what is notable about the "artificiality" of this procedure is that it characterizes not only cinema but also philosophy, language, and even our intelligence and our ways of perceiving (or perceptive habits). For this reason, as Bergson maintains, the cinematographic mechanism coincides with the mechanism of thought itself, and the new technology of nascent cinema merely corroborates the "oldest illusion" of conceptual thought (*CE*, 272/272).

There is not only a handy if surprising analogy between cinema and our oldest habits; they have a true common nature. Cinema exposes from the *outside,* so to speak, the most distinctive operation of human perception and intellect: they have a "cinematographical tendency" that is nothing less than our "natural metaphysic" (*CE*, 326/325–26). The operation of decomposing every singular becoming into a series of stable elements that are like snapshots or immo-

bile sections and then, after the fact, adding an abstract movement—
"becoming in general"—is, for Bergson, an artifice but an artifice
that is anything but arbitrary. In a reality always in becoming, always
in the process of being made and unmade, the living perceive only
halts and states, "snapshots" cut out from change. And the living are
right to do this: they must live, and to live they must act, and action demands a restrained perception that can select from the real
that which has interest. Our language and intellect are no exception:
from this perspective, as Bergson insists, they, too, are oriented by
the necessity of acting to live.[5]

The privilege of the stable over the unstable, and of the immobile over movement, thus emerges from an orientation toward action
that, in itself, is necessary and legitimate—at least within its own
limits, which are in fact overstepped from the outset. The habit of
taking instantaneous and immobile snapshots of the becoming of reality, and of retaining only what interests us in them in order to act,
quickly slips toward a "natural metaphysics" lodged in language but
also already lodged in the senses and the intellect. This habit leads us
to conceive of movement and change merely as accidents that happen to things that are by nature stable.[6] Aristotle's logic of predica-
tive judgment, which attributes a predicate (accident) to a subject
(substance), is the definitive expression of the power of this habit,
according to Bergson. But then an illusion takes hold. Not only do
we forget that the stable is a section of becoming, but we fall into the
trap of believing that it is possible to "think the unstable by means of
the stable, the moving by means of the immobile" (*CE*, 273/273), and
to recompose movement with immobilities:

> Such is the contrivance of the cinematograph. And such is also
> that of our knowledge. Instead of attaching ourselves to the inner
> becoming of things, we place ourselves outside them in order to
> recompose their becoming. We take snapshots, as it were, of the
> passing reality, and, as these are characteristics of the reality, we
> have only to string them on an abstract becoming. . . . Perception,
> intellection, language so proceed in general. Whether we would
> think becoming, or express it, or even perceive it, we hardly do

anything else than set going a kind of cinematograph inside us. We may therefore sum up what we have been saying in the conclusion that *the mechanism of our ordinary knowledge is of a cinematographical kind.* (*CE,* 306/305; translation modified)

Thus the "cinematographic mechanism of thought" did not have to wait for the birth of cinema to get to work; at most, it found in cinema a suitable name. In short, to summarize with Deleuze, it is "as though we had always made cinema without realising it" (*CI,* 2/10; translation modified). And if we think about the way cinema proceeds, this art of images in movement is no more able to grasp movements as they are happening than our perception or our intellect. Cinema, then, would only present false movement. But what is true movement? What are its characteristics? Bergson's thesis is famous: movement cannot be reduced to the space covered. Identifying movement with the trajectory it has drawn leads to unresolvable paradoxes, which condemn us to grasping nothing about movement. The arguments Zeno of Elea used to prove the inexistence of movement already presupposed this identification of movement with space covered, which, according to Bergson, continues to operate in the whole history of philosophy, even as it is the very root of the impossibility of thinking movement. Why? Because movement is indivisible, whereas space covered is divisible. Or, more precisely, movement can be divided only by "changing its nature," by becoming another movement, whereas space covered is infinitely divisible, decomposable and recomposable at will, because it is homogenous. This becomes clear in the paradox of Achilles and the tortoise. If Achilles can never catch up with the tortoise, since his first step takes him to the point where the tortoise had previously been and so on, this is because of the erroneous presupposition that Achilles' step— and the tortoise's step—are arbitrarily divisible like the segments of a line. But, of course, this is not so: each step is in reality indivisible, and this is why Achilles has no problem whatsoever catching up with the tortoise in a few bounds.[7] Movements are indivisible as well as heterogeneous, whereas spaces covered are homogenous. Achilles' step and the tortoise's step may very well trace the same trajectory in space, but their movements follow different articulations.

Because of movement's indivisible and heterogeneous nature, any attempt to reconstitute it with positions in space and instants in time is doomed to failure. Once a movement has been carried out, one can, of course, consider its trajectory, section it into positions in space, and correlate these positions with instants. But what is obtained through such a procedure is a succession of immobile positions, on the one hand, and, on the other hand, a homogenous and abstract time—a spatialized time. The underlying presupposition is that what is true of the line that has been traced is also true of the movement, but even if we bring two instants or two positions infinitely close, movement will elude us: it always "slips through the interval" (*CE*, 308/307). This is because we find ourselves, from the outset, in the absurd position of believing that a series of immobilities can produce movement. Here Bergson is denouncing an illegitimate spatialization of movement that implies the spatialization of time itself. Movement is reduced to space when it is made to coincide with a juxtaposition of points, and time is reduced to a series of instants that merely reproduces the spatial juxtaposition. But real, indivisible, and heterogeneous movement happens in a qualitative time, in duration. Deleuze summarizes this opposition with two formulas: on the one hand, we have "immobile sections + abstract time" and, on the other hand, "real movement + concrete duration" (*CI*, 1/10). We are now in a better position to understand why Bergson grants such significance to cinema as the paradigm of the "mechanism of thought." Photograms are instantaneous snapshots, "immobile sections," of positions or states that have been arbitrarily cut out from the real movement, which is unreeled over the length of an abstract and always identical time: the time "in" the projection apparatus. Rather than placing oneself within a singular movement and grasping its nature, one artificially decomposes and recomposes it.

Yet with respect to Deleuze's initial problem, that of finding the specificity of the movement of cinematographic images, Bergson's famous thesis does not seem to get us very far. Cinema as false movement is clearly not the answer Deleuze is seeking. But according to Deleuze, Bergson proposes not one but three theses on movement. The irreducibility of movement to space covered should not stop us from considering the other two theses and, above all, the way they are connected, which is what will allow Deleuze to give a cinematographic reading of Bergson and to bring out an "objective alliance" between Bergson and cinema. Because the whole project of *Cinema 1* depends on this alliance, its content needs to be defined.

Deleuze understands Bergson's distinction between the Ancients and the Moderns as a second thesis on movement. If both modern science and Greek metaphysics and science share the illusion that movement can be recomposed with instants or positions, they carry out this recomposition according to divergent principles and thus "miss movement" in two very different ways. Whereas Greek philosophy is a philosophy of ideas, which retains only privileged moments of movement-forms, modern science is built on the renunciation of any idea of form and considers movement in relation to any-instant-whatever. Art is no stranger to this difference in attitude; to the contrary. Bergson's example is a galloping horse; the Parthenon sculptors fix this gallop into a characteristic form that is meant to recapture the essence of the movement, whereas instantaneous photography isolates the gallop in any-instant-whatevers and decomposes it into any number of different positions. This is the distinction that we have already encountered between the ideal synthesis of movement and its sensible analysis. Cinema clearly belongs in the latter category, falling within the province of modern science and metaphysics. Then why, asks Deleuze, does Bergson project cinema backward, using it to express the commonalities of the ancient and modern manners of mistaking movement, rather than situating it, as would seem more legitimate, at their point of divergence, and understanding cinema as the exemplary evidence of the modern illusion? The reason for this, according to Bergson, is that ancient and modern sciences end up with the same result. The difference that separates them, as radical as it may be in some respects, is a difference "of degree rather than of kind" (*CE,* 332/332). To understand Bergson's position, we must take the nature of time into account more explicitly than we have done up to this point. If the philosophy of ideas retains only forms of movement while modern science is interested in the any-instant-whatever, this is because the first is essentially static, and time intervenes only as a degradation of eternity. Modern science, to the contrary, introduces time as an independent variable. Kepler and Galileo establish a new scientific paradigm, in Kuhn's sense, in which time becomes an essential element.[8] Bergson notes that Kepler's question—how to calculate the respective positions of planets at any moment whatever, once their position at a given moment is known—becomes the ideal problem of all science. Henceforward it will be a matter, at least in principle, of determining the relative positions of the elements of each material system as a function of time as an independent variable. There would seem to be a radical difference between a static science, in which time intervenes merely as degradation or as negligible interval between the passage of one eternal form to another, and a science in which time is the very element of all becoming and of all possible change, especially for Bergson, who sees the problem of becoming as the decisive problem of philosophy. Why, then, does Bergson nonetheless see the difference between modern science and ancient science as merely a difference of degree rather than kind?

Because there is not just one concept of time, and everything depends on how we understand its nature. As Deleuze rightly emphasizes, Bergson's central question concerns the production of the new, and philosophy must be converted from seeking out the eternal to analyzing what makes it possible for the new to appear (*CI*, 3/11). Time is this "condition of possibility"; nothing new is created without taking time. We may know a painter, his manner, model, and the colors he uses; nonetheless, Bergson remarks, we cannot foresee what will appear on the canvas, "that unforeseeable nothing which is everything in a work of art. And it is this nothing that takes time" (*CE*, 341/340). There is a time necessary to creation in art but in other domains as well: in history, society, and life itself.[9] But the time in question is time as duration, incessant qualitative change; time is not an external frame in which events occur but is identical with invention itself. It is this conception that leads Bergson to make the startling assertion that "time is invention or it is nothing at all" (*CE*, 341/341). Now, the time that coincides with the production of the new is precisely the kind of time that modern science ignores. For modern physics, as for Aristotle, time is the "number of movement," the movement of a mobile *T* on a trajectory that represents what is aptly called the "course of time."[10] Time thus draws a line in which purely temporal succession is copied from spatial juxtaposition. But because juxtaposition in space is de jure instantaneous, this spatialization of time is the origin of the illusion that everything in the universe is already given, that the future is, at least in principle, already contained in the present and the past, and that the whole of time could be unfolded instantaneously. Laplace's demon, who, knowing the position and speed of all particles in the universe at a given moment, could therefore know every future and past event, is the perfect expression of the consequences of understanding time as unfolding in space. De jure if not de facto, such time produces nothing; it is merely the abstract and ultimately inessential frame in which one event succeeds another without this succession affecting the nature of events in any way.[11]

It is in this reduction of time to a spatial model that ancient metaphysics and modern physics coincide, according to Bergson. And it is for this reason that both are under the auspices of the "cinematographic mechanism of thought," the true significance of which we are now in a position to understand. Not only does cinema extract "immobile sections" from movement, to which it then adds the abstract time of the movement of the camera, but, worse yet, in so doing it perpetuates the illusion that temporal succession is only the unfolding of spatial juxtaposition, which is negligible de jure. It leads us to believe that time is nothing but the artificial setting into motion of a whole that is already given at once "as on the film of the cinematograph" (*CE*, 339/339). Cinema, like thought, misses movement when it claims to reconstitute it with immobile shots that it unreels over the length of an abstract becoming rather than grasping the heterogeneity of movements as they are happening. At the same time, cinema, like thought, also misses time by retaining only that aspect that is copied from space: length-time, time as number of movement. Cinema, like thought, ignores a—fundamental—dimension of time: invention-time. Yet invention-time is necessary. In Bergson's terms, if succession is inevitable, if the future is condemned to succeed the present rather than being given at once, this is because time is identical to the unpredictable and the new, because "the duration of the universe must . . . be one with the latitude of creation which can find place in it" (*CE,* 340/339). What prevents time from being reduced to space is nothing other than its power of creation. Modern physics is no more able than ancient metaphysics to think this dimension of time. But even as he dismisses these two different but convergent forms of the spatialization of time, Bergson seems to feel some regret. The Ancients were interested in immobile essences; for them time is merely the degradation of the essence. But modern science no longer recognizes privileged instants, and "change is no longer a diminution of essence, duration is not a dilution of eternity" (*CE,* 344/343). Rather, modern science is situated from the outset within the flux of time, which becomes reality itself. This kind of science should be able to envision time as creation, and if it does not think it itself, it nonetheless calls for a "new philosophy."

Bergson thus seems to hesitate between two paths: gathering the Ancients and the Moderns under the same illusion, or insisting on the difference that separates them and on the need to produce a new philosophy for a science that can no longer accept a metaphysics of eternal ideas. Moreover, the very fact that Bergson uses nascent cinema to name "the oldest illusion" is, according to Deleuze, both sign and consequence of this hesitation. A descendant of instantaneous photography and of the immanent analysis of movement, cinema is lodged at the center of modern science. Why give such a new name to Zeno's paradoxes? Perhaps modern physics needs a new art, just as it needs a new philosophy. And perhaps cinema is one of these new art forms. And perhaps, even as he gives the name "cinema" to the illusion that must be overcome, what Bergson is saying about movement is in profound harmony with cinema. But in order to support this hypothesis and give coherence to his cinematographic reading of Bergson, Deleuze needs Bergson's third thesis on movement.

We have already seen why Bergson maintains that movement, which is indivisible and heterogeneous, is irreducible to space covered, which, to the contrary, is divisible and homogenous. This is the first thesis. The second thesis, as we have just seen, concerns the different methods the Ancients and Moderns used to reconstitute movement with instants or positions. As for the third thesis, we have already encountered it without explicitly naming it. The third thesis asserts that *the whole is not given*. Of course, as Bergson formulates it, this thesis bears directly on time and only indirectly on movement. But Deleuze links the three theses together according to a logic in which movement and time are indissociable. Deleuze himself produces this linkage; it is never explicitly formulated in Bergson's text. It is, strictly speaking, Deleuze's cinematographic reading of Bergson: it allows one to grasp a coherence in Bergson's position that often goes unnoticed and is the force behind the whole analysis of cinema that Deleuze develops. We must therefore follow it attentively.

If movement cannot be reduced to space covered, and thus cannot be reconstituted with "immobile sections + abstract time," this is because movement as translation in space is inseparable from a change in duration. For Bergson, as we know, duration is qualitative change, or pure becoming. And duration, as we know, which Bergson initially saw as psychological and identical to consciousness, will take on an ontological dimension in the texts after *Time and Free Will: An Essay on the Immediate Data of Consciousness*. Bergson comes to view duration as the opening of time as change, the opening of the universe or being. Bergson often calls this dimension the Whole. But, Deleuze insists, we should not mistake the Whole for a closed set; it is itself the Open, the dimension of a time-being that changes and, in changing, endures and produces the new.[12] If movements are qualitative and heterogeneous, it is because they participate in the Whole of the universe. They express a change in the Whole. Each translation in space is an affection of duration: "An animal moves, but this is for a purpose: to feed, migrate, etc." (*C1,* 8/18; see *MM* 111/121). Space and duration, movement as translation and movement as qualitative change, are thus not only irreducible but interrelated. The Whole as open is precisely what allows Deleuze to establish this relation and to give a more "rigorous" status to Bergson's theses. Rather than simply opposing the two formulas "immobile sections + abstract time" and "real movement + concrete duration," the first expressing an illusion and the second a real relation, they are now related to two different systems. The first formula applies to closed sets, systems that consist of a certain number of distinct parts, material systems that are spread in space, like those systems that modern physics was able to isolate. In such systems one can, in fact, consider immobile sections and calculate successive states as a function of abstract time. The second formula refers, on the contrary, to an open Whole that endures and continues to change.

But one cannot stop with this distinction. Sets are only artificially closed; they participate in the open. Movement is what produces the passage between two levels. Rather than distinguishing "false" from "true" movement, Deleuze suggests that it be considered from two aspects. On the one hand, movement is an effect of translation: it establishes itself between the objects of closed sets and modifies their respective positions. On the other hand, but inseparably, it expresses duration or the Whole. In this way movement relates "the objects of a closed system to open duration and duration to the objects of the system which it forces to open up" (*C1*, 11/22). Movement of translation and change in duration are identical. The objects of a closed system can be considered as immobile sections, and the movement established between them can be considered as a mobile section of duration. In other words, movement is a mobile section of time. Why is this term or concept important? What are its implications for philosophical conceptions of time and movement? And, above all, since this is Deleuze's purpose, how does it relate to cinema? Our point of departure was the need to think the specificity of cinema, the singular concepts that cinema demands. And once again we are confronted with speculations on the nature of movement and time that have no apparent link to films. We can only answer this set of questions progressively, but we will soon see an initial relation to cinema come into focus.

In effect, the concept of the mobile section allows Deleuze to establish a connection between movement and image. Deleuze is still referring to Bergson, but this time to the Bergson of the first chapter of *Matter and Memory.* In this chapter, which we will have occasion to revisit, Bergson discovered a type of images that differ from those static images that are instantaneous and immobile snapshots of movement: images that do not resemble the photograms of cinematographic films but that are movement from the outset and in themselves. Drawing a parallel with Einstein's physics, Bergson in effect proposes a conception of the material universe as a universe of figures of light and movement, "blocs of space-time," as Deleuze often puts it. In this universe there would be an absolute coincidence between matter, light, and movement, and Bergson's name for this coincidence is "image": the material universe is a universe of moving images.[13] Or, more precisely, of *movement-images.* Deleuze introduces this term, which does not figure in Bergson, in order to underline an essential aspect of Bergsonian images: their mobility is absolute, so to speak, and does not depend on a mobile body as its substrate. And the term also, of course, establishes the connection with cinema since, according to Deleuze, it is precisely such movement-images that cinema and cinema alone produces. We will soon see why.

For Deleuze, the concept of the mobile section corresponds exactly to the movement-images of *Matter and Memory,* and by bringing it to bear on *Creative Evolution*'s thesis on movement, he is able to draw out a coherent linkage between images, time, and movement. Alongside instantaneous images, immobile sections of movement, there are also movement-images that are mobile sections of duration. Thus, image is not only on the first side of movement, the side turned toward the translation in space of objects that belong to closed sets. Image is also on the second side of movement, the side turned toward change in duration. For our perception, which is used to grasping movements as displacements in space, it is not easy to conceive of images that, in spatial translation itself, directly present a qualitative change, mental or spiritual: a change in the whole. At least, this was not easy before cinema, for, according to Deleuze, cinematographic images directly present the two sides of movement. In addition to these two types of images, Deleuze describes a third type at the end of the first chapter of *Cinema 1:* time-images, images capable of presenting duration and change directly, beyond movement. This anticipates *Cinema 2* and another type of cinema. But before we can grasp its significance, we need to analyze movement-images.

How is a film made? Through the choice of frames, the filming of the shots, and the montage of what has thus been obtained. The frame, the shot, and montage—realities familiar to any spectator of cinema, even to one who has no desire or concern for theory—are simultaneously the basic operations in the making of a film and the concepts fundamental to any cinematographic analysis, for historians and critics of cinema, of course, but first and foremost for filmmakers themselves. It is not surprising, therefore, to find great differences in the various theoretical and practical approaches to these basic notions. Deleuze's definitions are closely connected to the history of cinema, often derived from films themselves, and in constant dialogue with the most important works of cinematographic criticism. But if Deleuze clearly has an intimate knowledge of cinema and its theories, one should not mistake the status of his discourse. However important certain critical currents might be, and however they influenced him, Deleuze inserts the elements he derives from them into another line of thought, one that often displaces the very terms of the debate and gives his approach its originality.

Let us begin with the frame. The operation of framing determines the set of elements present in the image (props, characters, sets, etc.). The frame can thus be defined as a provisionally closed system, a set containing a large number of parts. These elements belong to the cinematographic image and can be counted. From this perspective, an initial aspect of the frame is its tendency toward saturation or, to the contrary, toward rarefaction. With the introduction of the technique of depth of field, in the work of Wyler and Welles, the number of elements in a single frame could, for instance, be multiplied to the point that the primary scene unfolds in the background while what we see in the foreground is a secondary scene. The opposite tendency—toward rarefaction—is a common procedure in Antonioni or Ozu, whose frames are emptied of nearly all their elements. Taken to its limit, rarefaction is the empty set, the black or white screen; Deleuze gives the example of the famous scene in Hitchcock's *Spellbound* (1945) in which the glass of milk invades the screen. The frame, with its saturated or rarified images, is a surface on which information—visual and sound information—is recorded. Deleuze insists that images are given not just to be seen but also to be read. But one should not be too quick to conclude that cinema and language are equivalent on the basis of the image's informational value. To the contrary: one of the major claims of *Cinema 1* and *2* is that filmic images are indeed signs, but they are not linguistic signs. Attempting to read cinema with structural linguistics is a trap that leads one away from the logic proper to images. This is why, already in the preface to *Cinema 1,* Deleuze places Peirce next to Bergson as the second major point of reference of his project. In fact, Deleuze will systematically return to Peirce's logic, which he sees as an alternative to Saussurean linguistics, as he develops a classification of cinematographic images.

Still other aspects of the frame must be taken into account. The frame is either geometric or physical. By the geometric frame, Deleuze means the conception that the limits of the frame preexist the objects that will be inserted within it. Antonioni is once again the paradigmatic example: his characters enter and leave frames that preexist them. A dynamic frame, on the other hand, is constructed around the power and movements of bodies that occupy it. We are thus confronted with two divergent conceptions of the limit: a geometric limit that precedes the existence of the bodies and fixes their essence, or a physical limit determined by the power of existing bodies. The third aspect of the frame is that it necessarily refers to an angle of framing, a point of view on the set. The history of cinema is punctuated by unusual and disconcerting points of view: at ground level, from high to low, from low to high, etc. Usually these extraordinary points of view have a pragmatic justification: they can be explained through a relation to a more comprehensive set or to an element in the scene that was not initially visible. The strangeness of the point of view is thus justified in the linkage of sequences. But there are also frames presenting a point of view whose abnormality cannot be erased by any pragmatic rule, such as the faces cut by the edge of the screen in Dreyer's *Passion of Joan of Arc*. To describe this type of frame, Deleuze borrows Pascal Bonitzer's concept of "deframing" [*décadrage*].[14] The visual image is thus confirmed to have a legible function, beyond its visible function.

In any case, what is seen through the image itself always opens onto the nonvisible. If framing's operation is to choose the elements present in the image, it necessarily gives the limits to this very image. But what do the limits of the frame open on to? This is how Deleuze poses the question of the out-of-field [*hors-champ*], which implies from the outset that the out-of-field is not, as is often thought, a particular technique that corresponds to one type of framing but not to others. According to Deleuze, there is never a frame without an out-of-field because the out-of-field refers to the necessary presence of "what is neither heard nor seen" (*C1*, 16/28; translation modified). This presence does, however, have different modes, which are, in effect, determined by the type of framing. To simplify, take two extreme cases: the frame conceived as the extraction of a set from a more comprehensive but homogenous set with which it communicates, and the frame conceived, to the contrary, as a closed space that tends to neutralize and exclude anything that exceeds it. Renoir's cinema, on the one hand, and Hitchcock's, on the other, are good examples of these two conceptions. In the first type of frame there is no doubt that an out-of-field is present. The frame extracts a part of space from a wider set, which it evokes positively and which will in turn become visible in the successive reframings. For Deleuze this is the first level that he had isolated in his interpretation of *Creative Evolution:* the level of closed material systems. But because the divisibility of matter implies that the sets constituted will never cease dividing themselves into subsets or joining up with more comprehensive sets, the system is only provisionally closed. Any point whatever in the universe can be attached to any other point whatever: "There is always a thread to link the glass of sugared water to the solar system" (*C1*, 16/29). The out-of-field in this first type of frame thus points at the continual communication between closed systems, to the "thread of the universe" that links one set to another in space.

But the second type of frame, which tends to neutralize any environment, no less presents an out-of-field; only, it is another kind of out-of-field, according to Deleuze, who on this point departs from the usual analyses of film. Material sets, as we have seen, continually divide and rejoin each other in order to form a Whole that itself has no closure. Material systems are linked to other systems in space, "integrated" into a Whole that transmits a duration to them. Framings that aim to exclude every spatial outside thus bear witness to an absolute out-of-field that, "out" of space and homogenous time, is of the order of duration or spirit. The deframings [*décadrages*] without pragmatic justification, mentioned above, likewise gesture toward this absolute out-of-field. Dreyer's two-dimensional images—his faces cut off by the screen—close off space in order to open themselves to time and to spirit, to Joan's decision in *Joan of Arc,* for instance. Rather than distinguishing between frames with or without an out-of-field, Deleuze thus distinguishes two aspects of the out-of-field itself: one that is relative, adding space to space, and one that is absolute, opening the image to immanent duration, to the whole of the universe. These aspects continually blend together, like matter and time, yet one nevertheless always prevails over the other:

> The thicker the thread which links the seen set to other unseen sets the better the out-of-field fulfils its first function, which is the adding of space to space. But, when the thread is very fine, it is not content to reinforce the closure of the frame or to eliminate the relation with the outside. It certainly does not bring about a complete isolation of the relatively closed system, which would be impossible. But, the finer it is—the further duration descends into the system like a spider—the more effectively the out-of-field fulfils its other function which is that of introducing the transspatial

and the spiritual into the system which is never perfectly closed.
(*CI,* 17/30–31)

These remarks on the out-of-field are important to Deleuze's analysis. Even at the level of framing, the most elementary level of the composition of a film, the double aspect (absolute and relative) of the out-of-field already engages the essential relation that links movements in space with change in duration in a specifically cinematographic way. With the analysis of the shot, which takes over from the analysis of the frame, we will have our first explicit cinematographic definition of the concept of the movement-image.

The multiplicity of the types of shots in cinema has elicited a certain skepticism about the possibility of ever giving a coherent definition of the shot itself.[15] According to Deleuze, however, the great variety of its forms of composition does not prevent the shot from having a unity that is perfectly describable. In the early days of cinema, before the introduction of the mobile camera, the frame was defined in relation to a unique, frontal point of view: the point of view of the spectator. In this context, the shot was a purely spatial determination indicating the distance between the camera and the objects filmed, from the close-up to the long shot. At this stage, these first images produced by cinema are not by their nature different from those in the theater, for instance. They are what Deleuze calls *images in movement* and not yet movement-images. What is the difference? For Deleuze, the difference is dramatic. In primitive cinema, as in natural perception, movement depends on a body displaced through a space that is itself fixed. Movement remains attached to moving bodies; it does not emerge in itself. The emancipation of movement, its appearance in a pure state, so to speak, would come to be one of cinema's great achievements, but it would only happen progressively, with the introduction of the mobile camera and montage.[16] With these techniques, the shot stops being an immobile space in which bodies and objects may be displaced, always in relation to the same frontal point of view, as if on a theatrical stage.[17] The shot itself becomes mobile, able to show a generalized movement that can be extricated from bodies, which previously had seemed to be the only means of bearing movement. Where images in movement show the displacements of mobile objects in a fixed space, movement-images mix up spaces and release a pure mobility.

The shot's intermediary function in the construction of a film, between framing and montage, can be easily explained, according to Deleuze, if one considers it as a mobile section. The shot, like all movement, has two aspects: on one side, it modifies the respective positions of the parts of a set (determined by the frame), and it thus establishes translations in space; on the other side, it expresses a change in the duration of the Whole, as an affection or articulation of duration (determined by montage). These two aspects are inseparable; unless it is totally arbitrary, the smallest displacement in a frame expresses a change that is happening. It follows that the shot as mobile section is a temporal perspective. In *What Is Cinema?* Bazin had already noted that if photography captures the "luminous impression" of an object, cinema manages to realize the paradox of "mak[ing] an imprint of the duration."[18] According to Deleuze, if the shot is able to extract from bodies the mobility that is their essence, just as Bergson wanted, it is precisely insofar as the shot is a mobile section of duration:

> The shot is the movement-image. In so far as it relates movement to a whole which changes, it is the mobile section of a duration. Describing the image of a street demonstration Pudovkin says: it is as if you climbed on a roof to see it, then you climb down to the first floor window to read the placards, then you mix with the crowd. . . . It is only "as if"; for natural perception introduces halts, moorings, fixed points or separated points of view, moving bodies or even distinct vehicles, whilst cinematographic perception works continuously, in a single movement whose very halts are an integral part of it and are only a vibration on to itself. . . . This was what Bergson wanted: beginning from the body or moving thing to which our natural perception attaches movement as if it were a vehicle, to extract a simple coloured "spot," the movement-image, which . . . "is in reality only a movement of movements." (*C1*, 22–23/36–37)

Bergson did not understand this power of cinema. A spectator of its beginnings, he could not, according to Deleuze, see its vocation of liberating movements and of producing new images. Yet the fact remains that, more than anyone else, Bergson was thinking what the cinema, on its side, was doing. Whence the "objective alliance" between Bergsonism and cinema, many consequences of which we still have to discover.

2 ■ Cinema and Perception

> We imagine perception to be a kind of photographic
> view of things, taken from a fixed point by that special
> apparatus which is called an organ of perception. . . .
> But is it not obvious that the photograph, if photograph
> there be, is already taken, already developed at the very
> heart of things, and at all points in space?
>
> Henri Bergson, *Matter and Memory*

In his famous 1938 essay "Die Zeit des Weltbildes," Heidegger gives a
powerful interpretation of the ontological status of images in modernity.[1] He describes the modern age as a double movement by which
man becomes subject at the same time as the world becomes image.
Man as subject and the world as image are the two faces of representation, which is the real ontological foundation of modernity.[2] What
is essential in this thesis, as Heidegger insists, is not the description
of modernity as an age that produces an image, a conception, or a
Weltanschauung of the world, which it indeed does, but rather the
assertion that the world itself, the world as such, has become image
because its essence is to be given to a subject in representation. The
world *is* as an object of representation of a subject:

> [W]orld image, when understood essentially, does not mean an
> image of the world but the world conceived and grasped as im-
> age.[3]

According to Heidegger, as we know, it is precisely insofar as modernity is the age of representation that it is also, inseparably, the
age of technics and science: as an object of representation, the world
becomes an object of calculation and mastery. The objectivity of sci-

ence is secured by the objectivity of representation: subjectivity and objectivity are the two faces of a single ontological condition. The becoming image of the world thus does not imply any relativism.

Cinema was certainly not one of Heidegger's important subjects.[4] Yet it would seem to be the perfect confirmation of his description of modernity. Halfway between art and industry, dependent on the development of technologies, cinema would be the "modern" art par excellence. Insofar as it shows an image-world to the gaze of a spectator-subject, it seems to reduplicate the ontological condition of modernity in a technological aesthetic.[5]

Now, for Deleuze, there is indeed a world of images but in an entirely different sense: a world of images in which cinema participates without reduplicating it in any way. It is a world of material images and diffuse perception, radically independent of any subjective representation, a world that is not modern, premodern, or postmodern because it is not as old as the epochs of Heideggerian being or as human history but as old as the universe. This kind of universe of images in themselves and for themselves, immanent images that wait for no human gaze, is what Bergson describes in the first chapter of *Matter and Memory*, "Of the Selection of Images for Conscious Presentation: What Our Body Means and Does."[6] And it is on the level of the status of images that the "objective alliance" between Bergson and cinema is forged. Although Bergson did not recognize the "essence and its promise" of nascent cinema, Deleuze views this as merely a minor fault, since he sees Bergson as the only one who elaborated an ontology of images that departs from that of the philosophical tradition while being in perfect harmony with cinema.

The problem Bergson describes in the first chapter of *Matter and Memory* is not exclusively his but one that he shares with a whole generation. The problem is how to overcome the classic opposition between the order of consciousness and the order of things, between materialism and idealism, between the project of reconstructing the order of consciousness from movements of the material universe and that of reconstructing the universe from representations of consciousness. The need to go beyond this dualism appears in a particularly acute form in the crisis affecting the psychology of the time, which *understood* consciousness as the receptacle of images, unextended and qualitative, and relegated movements, extended and quantitative, to space. As Deleuze notes, many scientific and social factors helped make this position untenable by placing "more and more movement into conscious life, and more and more images into the material world" (*C1*, 56/84). And, indeed, the two great projects for reviving philosophy at the beginning of the twentieth century—Bergson's and Husserl's—had the same point of departure: the necessity of filling the *gap* between consciousness and its images, on the one side, and the world and its things, on the other, and thus abandoning the dispute between idealism and materialism in order to rebuild philosophy on a ground closer to experience. But despite this shared necessity, Bergson and Husserl diverge so significantly that, according to Deleuze, their positions present a true alternative of thought. For Husserl, the bridge between consciousness and world does not have to be constructed because consciousness is always consciousness of something. All of phenomenology is *constituted* around this principle of intentionality, according to which consciousness cannot exist outside its relations with the objects at which it is aimed. In this case, the classic dualism can be exceeded through a philosophy of subjectivity, a re-elaborated concept of the transcendental subject.[7] For Bergson, on the contrary, there is no gap to be filled because consciousness *is* something.[8] What does this mean? And what are the consequences of this claim for an understanding of images?

Rather than starting from the subject or consciousness, Bergson places himself from the outset within a universe of images that have nothing in common with the old "mental images" of classical philosophy, since they coincide absolutely with movements. The universe that Bergson describes is a universe of images in themselves, which is based on a series of simple equivalences. The first of these is the equivalence of image and movement. Image is everything that appears, and in this Bergsonian world every thing—which is to say, every image—acts on and reacts immediately to everything else. There is not yet any distinction between received movement and executed movement: we are in the presence of a radically acentered universe, without axes, with neither left nor right, a world of "universal variation" (*C1*, 58/86).

But this first equivalence of image and movement entails another: that of image and matter. If images exist in themselves, if nothing is hidden behind them, this is because images are matter itself: movement-image and flowing-matter are one and the same. It is indeed a material universe, but, as Deleuze carefully explains, it is not a mechanistic universe because it is not a closed or finite system in which the only actions occur by contact. On the contrary, it is an infinite universe, on which closed systems are made and unmade, defined by Deleuze as a bloc of space-time or a plane of immanence.[9] But to understand its nature, the last equivalence must be introduced: the equivalence of image and light. The universe described by Bergson originates from the encounter between, on the one hand, a philosophical position that refuses to make consciousness or the subject the point of departure or arrival of experience and, on the other hand, Bergson's assessment of the importance of Einstein's theory of relativity. In fact, if one can speak of images in themselves, as Bergson does, of an appearing that is not addressed to anyone, without any spectator, it is for a negative reason: to distinguish images from what they have not yet become. Or more precisely, it is to distinguish them from what simultaneously constitutes the categories of our language and the objects of our perception: bodies (substantives), qualities (adjectives), actions (verbs). To speak of action implies that movement has already been substituted with the result it produces or the place it is directed to, just as speaking of quality implies the idea of a state that subsists, waiting for its possible replacement by another state; body, finally, replaces movement with the idea of a subject that carries it out, an object that submits to it, or a vehicle that carries it (*C1*, 59–60/88). Like our consciousness, such images are formed in the universe and exist there—we will see how—but they are not the whole of the universe.

Nonetheless, if images exist in themselves and appear without being for anyone, it is not only for this negative reason. The need to distinguish them from what they are not yet—consciousness and subjective perception—is not enough to justify the paradox of an image without gaze. There must be a positive reason for speaking of the being in themselves of images, a reason that Bergson finds in the fact that the universe is entirely light. The identity of image and movement thus implies another identity: that of matter and light. As will become more explicit in his later work *Duration and Simultaneity,* Bergson already implicitly recognizes in *Matter and Memory* the importance of the change of perspective that the theory of relativity will bring about in giving priority to light and energy over the solid bodies of a Euclidian universe.[10] After relativity, it is the line or "the figure of light which imposes its conditions on the rigid figure" (*CI,* 60/88, quoting Bergson). In the plane of immanence, light propagates itself in all directions, and movement-images, blocs of space-time, are figures of light in which rigid bodies are not yet formed. There is no eye to which such images can appear because light encounters neither obstacle nor screen to reflect it. But the notion of appearing in itself is no longer enigmatic: one now understands that "the eye is in things, in luminous images themselves," to use Deleuze's words, or, as Bergson puts it, that "photography, if there is photography, is already taken, already developed, at the very heart of things, and at all the points in space" (*CI,* 60/89).

In *L'imagination,* Sartre already highlighted the way Bergson performs a sort of inversion of the classic comparison; instead of seeing consciousness as a light that moves toward things, Bergson gives things a luminosity that invests the subject. Nonetheless, according to Deleuze, Sartre does not recognize the real importance of Bergson's move.[11] In Deleuze's eyes, Bergson is here breaking with the whole philosophical tradition, a claim that is all the more remarkable insofar as "the" philosophical tradition is not a standard locution in Deleuze's writing. Deleuze never shared the Heideggerian idea of an essential unity of the history of philosophy. Philosophy had always deemed light to be an attribute of spirit and considered consciousness "a beam of light which drew things out of their native darkness" (*CI,* 60/89). Phenomenology is merely the faithful continuation of this tradition, simply readjusted for its own time. Husserl's affirmation of the intentionality of consciousness, which is never isolated but always consciousness of something, is like opening an "internal light" on to the exterior, "rather as if the intentionality of consciousness was the ray of an electric lamp" (*C1*, 60/89). For Bergson, however, consciousness is a *thing*. De jure, it coincides with the set of light images and is immanent to matter; a de facto consciousness emerges from this plane of immanence when very special images—living images—form a "black screen" that can stop the infinite propagation of light and reflect it. Our de facto consciousness is merely an opacity that allows light to be revealed (*MM*, 39/36).

Before turning to these living images, of which we humans are a part, let me summarize the different aspects that define Bergson's universe, which Deleuze interprets in terms of a plane of immanence or matter: it is a set of movement-images, a collection of lines or figures of light, a series of blocs of space-time (*C1*, 61/90). Although the term *movement-image* does not appear in *Matter and Memory*, we can nonetheless grant to Deleuze that the concept, as introduced in regard to cinematographic images, is indeed present in the text: Bergson describes precisely a movement freed from any framework or anchoring in bodies. This is one of the reasons for claiming the "objective alliance" between Bergson and cinema, but it is not the only one. If we give further consideration to the equivalence of images not only with movement but with light and matter (the "blocs of space-time," whose great importance for cinema in Deleuze's view and for his whole aesthetic we will discuss below), we can consider such an equivalence to be a first and basic description of cinema. After all, what is cinema but a material set of images made of light, shadows, and movements? There is no shortage of such "minimalist" definitions of cinema nor of experiments along those lines in non-figurative cinema. But, contrary to what a certain Deleuzian *doxa* might lead one to expect, Deleuze is not content with this minimal description. Deleuze, indeed, sees Bergson's universe as a perfect *metacinema* but only when it has also given rise to "living images" and to everything that our ordinary perception sees and names: actions, affects, bodies. Only then will Deleuze institute a comparison between the universe of *Matter and Memory* and cinema as it is, or as it has mostly been: figurative and narrative. The encounter between philosophy and cinema can take place only with cinema and its history as we know them, not with a hypothetical or normative cinema, cinema as it should be or should have been, as it is not and has not been. The strength of *Cinema 1* and *2* comes largely from Deleuze's close engagement with films and filmmakers.

We still must understand how, in this radically acentered universe of continual variations and diffuse perceptions, centers are formed and conscious perception surges in images themselves. Bergson does not need to introduce different factors to explain the formation of perception in the ordinary sense of the term; for him, it is enough that an interval emerge between movements, that there be a gap between actions and reactions. Alongside images that react with each other in all their parts, there are particular images, living images or matters, with specialized facets. Some of these images merely receive actions, whereas others merely execute reactions. But this is not everything: the receptive facet of living images retains only some of the received excitations and allows all the others to pass through it. This facet thus isolates from all actions a small number of actions that interest it, and perception emerges from this operation of selection and isolation. In short, we perceive in the same way that a director determines a frame: by cutting out from the whole of the universe the part—variable, of course—that interests us.[12]

The isolating frame corresponds, on its other facet, to the temporal interval that prevents reactions from being linked immediately to the undergone actions. The gap between received movement and executed movement allows living images to choose their response and to act in the strict sense of the term. This is why Bergson calls living images "centers of indetermination": the impossibility of predicting an action coincides in this case with the possibility of creating the new.

The same process can be described in relation to the other characteristic of images: light. Bergson says that living images introduce into the plane of matter the black screen that the photograph was missing in order to be taken: rather than being propagated without resistance, light now encounters an obstacle, an opacity that reflects it. Perception is nothing other than the effect of the black screen, light reflected by a living image, and the brain, also an image, is nothing other than an interval between an action and a reaction. Rather than making the brain the mysterious receptacle of images, Bergson makes it one image among others on a plane of immanence that contains only light-matter and time (*MM*, 30/26). Deleuze is fascinated by Bergson's "principle of economy" and by this immanent universe, all the more so because time will be enough for him—as it is for Bergson, in a certain sense—to introduce the notion of spirit without reduplicating the material world with a transcendent one. We will return to this important point later.

Inseparably a center of indetermination and a black screen, the living image perceives insofar as it selects, as we have seen. It thus constitutes what Deleuze calls the first material level of subjectivity: *subtractive* subjectivity (*C1*, 63/93). But the perception-image is not limited to sorting; it incurves the universe around itself and gives a horizon to the world. This is the case because perception is merely one side of the gap, the other side of which is action. The living image subtracts what does not interest it from the thing, but what is interesting and what is not are relative values defined yet again and as always by the image's capacity for action. Perception shows us the usable face of things, whereas action teaches us how to use them.[13] Perception is thus always essentially sensorimotor and pragmatic, always oriented by and toward the needs and interests of life, as Bergson repeatedly maintains. The belief that perception's sole aim is pure knowledge, all too common in philosophy, is not merely an isolated error but also the origin of all sorts of false conceptions in metaphysics. Mistaking the nature of perception implies that the nature and limits of knowledge have also been mistaken. This central thesis of Bergsonism plays a fundamental role in Deleuze's thought in general and in his books on cinema in particular. Let us start to assess its consequences.

In the universe of movement-images, perception-images and action-images are formed. The operation of perception-images is framing; the operation of action-images, which constitute the second material aspect of subjectivity, is to incurve the universe, to measure "the virtual action of things on us and our possible action on things" (*CI, 65/95*). But what happens between perception and action, between the two sides of the gap? What is lodged in the interval? There must be something to establish a link between received movement and executed movement: between a perception, troubling in some respects, and a hesitant action, what surges is affection. The part of movements that is not transformed into objects of perception nor into acts becomes affection, the coincidence of the subject with itself or with the object, the "motor tendency" of an immobilized receptive facet (*CI, 65–66/96–97*). This is the affection-image, the third material aspect of subjectivity, which transforms the movement of translation into a movement of expression, into pure quality.

Within the acentered and perpetually varying universe of movement-images, three types of subjective images emerge: perception-images, action-images, and affection-images. The result of this is the formation of what Deleuze calls "a double system . . . of reference of images" (*CI, 62/92*). In the first system, all the images act on and react with each other in all their facets; in the second system, to the contrary, all the variations and changes are related to a single, living image that has specialized its facets and has become able to select received movements and executed movements. The thing and its perception are one and the same image; their difference is due to the system to which they are related. The thing is the image in itself, the image as it appears in the first regime of reference, perceiving itself and perceiving all the other images insofar as it submits to their actions. On the one hand, it is a "complete, immediate, and diffuse" perception (*CI, 63/94*). On the other hand, perception in the ordinary sense of the term—subjective perception—is the same image but now related to a special image that analyzes it and retains only a few of its aspects. Consciousness surges as a function of the needs of life; natural perception is formed within the objective and complete perception of things by becoming less keen, perceiving less, tracing in the continuity of movements and sensible qualities delimitations that are coarser but perfectly suited to the demands of what we call living (*MM*, 198/222).

Deleuze once again finds confirmation of what he sees as a line of absolute divergence between Bergson and phenomenology: phenomenology establishes subjective experience and natural perception as the model—even when, as in Merleau-Ponty, it grants that the subject is flesh and necessarily caught in the world—but for Bergson, to the contrary, natural experience and perception have no privilege whatsoever.[14] According to Bergson, philosophers are wrong to make experience coincide with subjective experience, only to note the fragility of such experience and then to draw the conclusion that any project of philosophical construction must be abandoned.[15] Their first error is to see perception as a pure function of knowledge, with no other finality than knowledge, thus ignoring its sensorimotor characteristics, which are turned toward action. If these characteristics are taken into account, another task is laid out for philosophy, that of a turn of experience able to go beneath or beyond its properly human moment:

> But there is a last enterprise that might be undertaken. It would be to seek experience at its source, or rather above that decisive turn where, taking a bias in the direction of our utility, it becomes properly human experience.[16]

Or, in the terser words of *The Creative Mind:* "Philosophy should be an effort to go beyond the human condition" (228/218). As early as 1966, Deleuze had recognized as a central motif in Bergsonism the claim that experience and thought are irreducible to the model of natural perception and to subjectivity in general. At the time, he wrote:

> Bergson is not one of those philosophers who ascribes a properly human wisdom and equilibrium to philosophy. To open us up to the inhuman and superhuman (durations which are inferior or superior to our own), to go beyond the human condition: This is

the meaning of philosophy, in so far as our condition condemns us to live among badly analyzed composites, and to be badly analyzed composites ourselves.[17]

Now, this irreducibility of experience to natural perception links Bergson and cinema in an *objective* alliance. For Deleuze, the material universe of movement-images is, strictly speaking, a metacinema, which allows him to go well beyond Bergson's explicit positions on cinema and to establish the comparison on a very different level. Likewise, cinema is just as irreducible to the model of natural perception. The mobility of the camera and the variability of angles of framing always reintroduce zones that are acentered and deframed in relation to any "perceiving subject" whatever. Cinema is closely related to the first regime of the movement-image, that of universal variation and total, objective perception. It has the power of undoing the "turn" where "experience becomes properly human" in order to return to perception in matter, to come back to the in-itself of the image.

Dziga Vertov's *cine-eye* testifies to this possibility, according to Deleuze. Perhaps the most experimental of Soviet filmmakers, Vertov radically refuses any idea of scenario or dramatic action and makes emphatic use of all kinds of "trick shots"—high-speed or slow-speed shots, microshooting, superimposition, deceleration, etc.—in order to realize the program of a materialist cinema. Vertov demands a kind of cinema that needs nothing but images, movements, and intervals (exactly like Bergson) to "put perception into matter," to link any point whatever in space with any other point, in order to attain the objectivity of "a seeing without boundaries or distances" (*C1*, 81/117).[18] In this kind of program, montage has a decisive function. If the camera can overcome certain limitations of the human eye, it is nonetheless subject to the same condition of possibility: as a receptive organ, the camera needs a certain immobility and organizes the variation of all images in relation to a privileged image.

In *Man with a Movie-Camera* (1929), his most famous film, Vertov constantly presents the relation between the human eye, the camera eye, and the interplay of several cameras that simultaneously show what is filmed and the machine that is filming. But this play of gazes, which always moreover implies the invisible camera, is not the moral of the film. It is not simply a matter of replacing the human eye with a technical eye; Vertov's project goes farther still: the vision he wants to attain is the vision in things. Montage can overcome the limits shared by the human eye and the camera eye; it can liberate vision from the mooring point that defines it and relate any point whatsoever in space to any other point.[19] This is what is so original, according to Deleuze, about Vertov's conception of the interval: rather than separating two consecutive images, the interval is what establishes a relation between two distant images that are "incommensurable from the viewpoint of our human perception" (*C1*, 82/118). Vertov does not limit himself to this single aspect of montage; he brings it into the images themselves and, in a sense, even into the photogram that becomes a decisive element in *Man with a Movie-Camera*. He is no longer content to reverse movement, as he had done by moving from dead meat to live flesh, for example; he now makes the photogram the genetic element of every movement and every possible perception (*C1*, 83/120). One may of course see a blatant contradiction between the interventionism of montage and the desire to recapture the real, as Jean Mitry does.[20] For Deleuze, however, there is no contradiction: the creativity of montage—its constructivism—is an operation necessary to cinema, as to all art, because what is at stake in art is never "reproducing the visible, but rendering visible," as Paul Klee puts it in a phrase that Deleuze often cites.[21]

But bringing the eye into matter is not cinema's sole power or sole vocation. It is also able—eminently able—to rise from the movement-image to its three varieties. The connection, or the assemblage [*agencement*], as Deleuze puts it, between perception-, action-, and affection-images constitutes the very matter of films. Moreover, the great majority of cinema, "classic" European cinema, as well as "classic" American and Soviet cinema, is structured around the action-image and a certain conception of montage. However great the differences between schools and directors, and they are indeed great, cinema has generally been shaped by the sensorimotor scheme of pragmatic perception[22] and conceives of montage as the only possible representation of time: an indirect image. Because the concept of an *indirect image of time* is central, let us grant it some attention.

We have already seen that the plane of movement-images is a "bloc of space-time." In more Bergsonian terms, this means that the plane itself is a perspective or a mobile section of time as the Whole, of time as duration. In other words, the plane should not be confused with time itself, of which it is a singular, and therefore not exhaustive, perspective. From this, Deleuze concludes, "We are therefore justified in thinking that there are time-images which are themselves capable of having all kinds of varieties" (*C1*, 68/101). And we will see how cinema is able to create all sorts of time-images, including *direct* time-images. For the moment, let us start with an analysis of the first type of time-images: indirect images of time, produced by the assemblage [*agencement*] and comparison of movement-images between themselves. In cinema, this relates to a conception according to which the presentation of time, of the Whole that changes, occurs only in the film as a whole and is thus dependent on montage. This is a powerful conception, which produced countless masterpieces in the history of cinema from Griffith to Pasolini, and we will return to it. According to Deleuze, this is the cinematographic equivalent of philosophies that think time as the number of movement.[23] In effect, montage as indirect image of time means both that time does not present itself directly in images, but only by means of their linkage, and—consequently—that time, in order to be shown, is dependent on movement.

Modern cinema, instead, is characterized by a different conception of montage, one that is strictly dependent on a different conception of the relation between time and image. According to this other idea of cinema, time pierces through the image itself directly and without the mediation of a succession of movement-images. Tarkovsky is an exemplary case: he is not only one of the great filmmakers but also one of the great theorists of a cinema of the time-image; Italian neorealism and André Bazin's powerful interpretation of it are other powerful instances of what Deleuze means by a cinema of time. We will return to these important questions in subsequent chapters, but even now it should be emphasized that, according to Deleuze, the possibility of a direct time-image emerges on the plane of movement-images, at the point where the "living image," "the centre of indetermination, which can avail itself of a special situation on the plane of movement-images, can itself have a special relationship with the whole, duration or time" (*C1*, 69/101). This first possibility allows us to glimpse the existence of images of many other types than those we have encountered up to this point.

Cinema, for Deleuze, is thus not limited to freeing movement; it is also able to explore for itself the "turn of experience" that Bergson so desired. It can undo the sensorimotor link of human perception both in order to go back toward the acentered universe of movement-images—toward matter not yet incurved by the human gaze—and to go beyond it toward dimensions of time, spirit, or thought freed from the demands of action and pragmatic perception, just as it can settle into the world of human actions and affects, though always with a little disruption.

But if the universe itself is the spatiotemporal assemblage [*agencement*] of movement-images, a veritable cinema in itself, how can we avoid the suspicion that cinema is merely the technical reduplication of an ontological condition? Of course, the ontology in question is very different from Heidegger's, but, after all, might not cinema occupy exactly the same place, that of a technological mirror of being? At first glance, this suspicion seems legitimate. It has even recently been put forward by Jacques Rancière.[24] Nonetheless, if we look more closely, cinema, as Deleuze understands it, is by no means a mirror and has nothing to reduplicate. Not only is the critique of the category of representation one of the most constant philosophical themes in Deleuze's thought,[25] but, where *Cinema 1* and *2* are concerned, it should be noted that cinematographic images, far from being the representation or copy of an ontological reality exterior to them, are images among others on *one and the same* plane of immanence.

If cinema is not the double of being, is it, then, an instrument in service of a revelation, the black plate that makes the photograph visible, as Bergson said of the living image? Deleuze does not categorically reject a certain use of religious terms,[26] but revelation is not one of his concepts. He prefers another Bergsonian theme: the creation of the new. The "turn of experience" of which cinema, in its greatest moments, is capable consists, of course, in the fact of undoing that which our habits, needs, and laziness have done, in order to make visible what the human eye is not made to see. But what cinema gives us to see are the perceptions, affects, and relations of thought that cinema itself was able to create. The "inhuman" task of philosophy and cinema, as of every art and every science, always consists in the fact of looking beyond or before, in any case of looking elsewhere than to that which is frozen in our habits of perception, sensation, and thought.[27]

The analysis of the affection-image, to which Deleuze devotes two important chapters in *Cinema 1,* is paradigmatic in this respect.[28] From the beginnings of cinema, the power of expressing affects was entrusted to the close-up, most often identified with the most expressive part of the human body: the face. Deleuze does not contest the equivalence of the affection-image with the close-up, but he reverses the meaning of its identification with the face. The close-up does not consist in enlarging or tearing an object from the set to which it belongs. Its operation is different: the close-up abstracts the object from all spatiotemporal coordinates and submits it to an absolute change rather than a simple change in dimensions, such that the movement is no longer one of *translation* but of *expression* (*C1,* 96/136). What is extracted from the space-time that surrounds it is a pure affect. But Deleuze does not see why such power of expression should be reserved for the face strictly speaking, more than any other part of the body or any object whatever. Deleuze thus proposes another thesis: "There is no close-up of the face. The close-up is the face" (*C1,* 99/141). This means that any object, extracted from its habitual spatiotemporal coordinates, can take on the power of expression that one generally ascribes to the face: "The 'edge,' the 'blade,' or rather the 'point' of Jack the Ripper's knife, is no less an affect than the fear which overcomes his features" (*CI*, 97/138). All the more so if one considers the fact that the face, strictly speaking, also expresses impersonal affects, as Epstein noted, and Deleuze cites: we see cowardice as such as soon as we see the close-up of a coward in flight.[29] The close-up is thus defined not by its relative dimensions but by its absolute dimension or its function, which is to express affect as entity, its being in itself that is independent and distinguishable from every person, every individualized state of things, and every determined space-time. This independence should be understood as the irreducibility of affects to anything but themselves, not as a lack of connection. A precipice may well explain an expression of terror, but it does not create it: the expression of affect exists in itself, and we do not need to see a precipice to understand terror. The two things are of a different order, and no possible causal relation could reduce their heterogeneity.[30] The impersonality of affects does not make them abstract but, on the contrary, gives them their singularity, just as their irreducibility to any determined space-time in no way prevents them from being the expression of a time and a space, of a determined epoch. This is why the new always emerges and why "new affects are ceaselessly created, notably by the work of art" (*CI*, 99/140).

Thus one regime of images does not reduplicate another but only offers a different perspective on the same plane of immanence. In contrast to modernity as described by Heidegger, the Bergsonian-Deleuzian universe has no subject that can become master of representation and fold the world that has become image around its gaze. The "subject" is one image among others; it does in fact give itself the horizon of a world and constitutes a "center of indetermination," but there are as many such centers as there are living images. This universe is a metacinema, but it should not be understood as a metatechnical universe. It is a universe of light-matter and blocs of space-time that is older than the history of living beings, older than the history of the technology that unfolds in it. Deleuze does not envisage the universe as a great machine; rather, what is at stake for him is a certain way of "naturalizing" cinema. Already in the preface to *Cinema 1,* he asserts that his study, in effect, is not a "history of the cinema" but a "taxonomy, an attempt at the classification of images and signs" along the lines of Linnaeus's natural history or Mendeleyev's chemistry (*C1,* xiv/7).[31] Yet it cannot be denied that human history actively intervenes in this taxonomy as that which articulates the passage from one type of cinematographic images and signs to another in the postwar period.[32] We will therefore need to interrogate the status of the intervention of history, asking if it introduces a tension or even a contradiction in the project of a "natural" classification of images, or if Deleuze can extend the dimensions of a certain kind of naturality to include human history proper.

3 ∎ *The Montage of the Whole*

The shot as movement-image, as we have seen, has two faces: one turned toward framing, which establishes the movement of translation between parts in space, the other turned toward montage, which expresses an absolute change in duration. Montage is thus charged with presenting time as the qualitative change of the Whole. Through continuities, false continuities, and cuts, montage determines the connection between movement-images. But if montage becomes the veritable *idea* of film, as Eisenstein would have it, this is because of a presupposition shared by so many theorists of montage, often great directors themselves, up to and including Pasolini: the presupposition, namely, that the idea of a film expresses a Whole that changes, a Whole that has changed, but one that can be grasped only through the connection of movement-images, through that operation proper to montage. In other words, because no image in itself seems able to express time, time must be deduced indirectly from the relations between images. Whence Deleuze's thesis that "Montage is composition, the assemblage [*agencement*] of movement-images as constituting *an indirect image of time*" (*C1*, 30/47; emphasis added).

To be precise, the time at issue here is the Whole in Bergson's sense of the open, the sense of qualitative duration as the incessant creation of the new. Note also that this conception of montage is not the only one that cinema has produced; in *Cinema 2,* Deleuze will analyze other forms of montage as they relate to the emergence of a new type of cinematographic image that presents time directly. But for the moment let us focus on "classical" montage and its methods of the indirect presentation of time. Because this is done with movement-images, Deleuze insists on an analogy between montage and all philosophical positions that think time as a function of movement; just as there are different ways of conceiving the relation between time and movement, there are different ways of conceiving montage as a composition of movement-images. Deleuze, of course, does not aim at "deducing" a grid of cinematographic possibilities (and impossibilities) from philosophy. On the contrary, he shows how different forms of creation encounter the same problems within their own domains. This is but one example of Deleuze's initial claim, in the preface to *Cinema 1,* that the power of thought proper to filmmakers is not based in a didactic use of cinema but is expressed in images themselves.[1]

Deleuze distinguishes four major trends that share similar sets of questions, notwithstanding the singularity of the films and directors: the organic trend of the American school; the dialectic trend of the Soviet school; the quantitative trend of the prewar French school; and, finally, the qualitative trend of German expressionism. For our purposes, we will consider only a few aspects of Deleuze's often detailed analyses and focus, namely, on his discussion of films by Griffith and Eisenstein. Our emphasis does not reflect any criterion of aesthetic value but pertains, rather, to the crucial role played by Griffith's organico-active and Eisenstein's organico-dialectic concepts of montage in the economy of Deleuze's undertaking and to their decisive importance in the history of cinema.

If Griffith is justifiably credited with having given montage its distinctive character, the form of montage that he actually fashioned is that of a powerful *organic* representation. Griffith's procedures are well-known: *parallel alternate montage,* in which the image of one part of the set succeeds another according to a certain rhythm, with the parts understood as being governed by binary relations (men and women, blacks and whites, the city and the country, the rich and the poor, etc.); *the insertion of the close-up;* and *concurrent or convergent montage,* the alternation between images of two different actions that will finally come together—or miss each other, if the junction takes place too late (*C1,* 30ff/47ff). These procedures are by no means purely technical; according to Deleuze, they express a conception of the assemblage [*agencement*] of movement-images as "an organisation, an organism, a great organic unity" (*C1,* 30/47). Alternate montage expresses the essential nature of every organism, namely, difference within unity. Men and women, north and south, exterior and interior, and so forth, are the diverse elements that compose an organic unity. The close-up, too, has a precise function, that of putting part and set into relation. Far from limiting itself to enlarging the detail, the close-up establishes a relation between a character's subjective gaze and the objectivity of the set: this is how the alternation between close-ups of soldiers and long shots of the battle works in *The Birth of a Nation* (1915), for example. Finally, convergent montage expresses another truth of the organic unity: that this unity is always threatened. The parts of a set "act and react on each other," some entering into conflict in order to destroy the unity, others joining forces to defend and restore it (*C1,* 30/47). Convergent montage shows two series of actions that will finally come together to face each other in the final confrontation, according to an increasingly rapid rhythm *(accelerated montage).* The form that Griffith gives to the combat within an organic unity is the *duel,* the personal face-off between the traitor and the righteous man (whether between individuals or the representatives of groups, it does not matter in this regard).

With these three forms of montage, Griffith could create an extremely powerful organic representation, capable of establishing a relation between the set and its parts even when the set in question becomes immense. In *Intolerance* (1916), Griffith, in effect, exceeds the already imposing frame of an entire nation to show the organic unity of a thousand years of the history of civilizations, from Babylon to contemporary America, which Deleuze summarizes as follows:

And the convergent actions are not just the duels proper to each civilisation—the chariot-race in the Babylonian episode, the race between the car and the train in the modern episode—but the two races themselves converge through the centuries in an accelerated montage which superimposes Babylon and America. Never again will such an organic unity be achieved, by means of rhythm, from parts which are so different and actions which are so distant. (*C1,* 31/49)

What, then, is the indirect image of time that Griffith gives us? Deleuze points out that whenever time has been thought as the measure of movement, it presents two complementary aspects that must be confronted: on the one hand, time as a whole, a circle, or a spiral that gathers together the movements of the universe, and, on the other hand, time as an interval, the smallest unit of the measure of movement. As we will see, there are several ways of conceiving these two aspects of time. Griffith, on Deleuze's reading, sees the set of movements in the universe as "the bird which hovers, continually increasing its circle," whereas the beating of a wing is the interval between two movements:

Time as an interval is the accelerated variable present, and time as whole is the spiral open at both ends, the immensity of past and future. . . . What originates from montage, or from the composition of movement-images, is the Idea, that indirect image of time: the whole which winds up and unwinds the set of the parts in the famous wellspring of *Intolerance,* and the interval between actions which gets smaller and smaller in the accelerated montage of the races. (*C1,* 32/50)

According to Deleuze, Griffith's montage came to serve as an archetype for American cinema, which, in its most "solid" form, was *organico-active.* Before clarifying this concept, I should perhaps stress that Deleuze in no way underestimates the importance and the inventive power of American cinema. The classification of images that he proposes is not, of course, intended to be hierarchical, and, as Deleuze insists, it does not correspond de jure to any criterion of value. But if this is the case, it is because a selection had already been made: only great directors and great films constitute the history of cinema, and there is no place for hierarchies among them.

We have just seen in what respects Griffith's montage is organic, but why does Deleuze further qualify it as *active?* Because the form it gives to the Whole of the film is one that moves from a general situation, given at the outset, to a restored or transformed situation at the end, by way of a series of actions that converge in the final duel. It is easy to recognize here the basic structure of the "action film," repeatedly played out even in its most recent avatars, thus attesting to the fact that Griffith's relevance extends beyond an archaeology of cinema. What Deleuze wants to show—and this is a crucial point in his analysis—is that this form is not the product of a subordination of cinema to narrativity, as is often claimed; on the contrary, it is narration that derives from this conception of montage. Why? And, above all, why is this order of priority so important?

From a negative or polemical perspective, the stakes are easy to understand (and, indeed, articulated explicitly): Deleuze aims to challenge the possibility of applying the model of structural linguistics to film and, more specifically, to contest Christian Metz's assimilation of the cinematographic image to an utterance, the assimilation that underlies the whole project.[2] According to Deleuze, it is incorrect to draw the conclusion, as Metz does, that narration itself is an evident given [*donnée apparente*] of images on the grounds of the historical fact that American cinema was shaped as narrative cinema. The evident given of images is movement, and the so-called "classical" narrative ensues from the organic composition of movement-images, just as modern forms of narration derive from the composition of another type of image, time-images.

Deleuze's suspicion of linguistics and psychoanalysis is not the only reason for his commitment to showing that the logic of images cannot be reduced to the logic of narration. Even more important, the problem with making narration a given of the image and of assimilating the image to an utterance is Bergson's problem of overly broad concepts taking the place of the real, the possible, and even the impossible. In other words: the problem is with a philosophical and theoretical attitude to generalization that misses the specificity of its objects of inquiry (Bergson, *Creative Mind,* 9/3). On this view, one looks "behind" images for their underlying structure, thus blinding oneself to what images are in themselves.[3] In short, assimilating cinema to a language is the best way to bypass cinema's singularity, the *singular essence* that Deleuze aims to describe, even if this means creating concepts that apply to cinema, and cinema alone.

But Deleuze is not only distancing himself from a model of cinematographic analysis that he deems unsuitable and even deceptive. The real issue is Deleuze's conception of cinema itself. Films are made from different types of images and from different forms of the composition of images, and nothing more. In other words, images and their composition are the sole essence of cinema, its singular essence. What must be grasped are cinema's own characteristics, rather than something behind or beneath it that would be its hidden structure, because *there is nothing* behind images, as Bergson tells us. Everything is in the images: Griffith's montage organizes movement-images by privileging the sensorimotor scheme that links perception and action and makes affection emerge between the two. Cinematographic narration follows the rules of this organico-active composition of images.

Eisenstein was fully aware of these aspects of Griffith's montage. As Deleuze remarks, while Eisenstein acknowledges his debt to Griffith, he criticizes Griffith's "bourgeois" conception of cinema, which is embodied directly in the form of montage rather than in the ideological content of the narrated stories (even when the content would easily lend itself to such criticism). Griffith's parallel and convergent montage alternates between the different parts of a set as independent phenomena that coexist alongside each other: the rich and the poor, blacks and whites, etc. It is thus no surprise that when these parts enter into conflict, the reasons are always personal and take the form of the duel. Even when whole groups are in opposition, the collective motives of the conflict are always superficial: they are merely the instruments of individual passions (love, desire for power, etc.). In short, Griffith has an entirely empirical idea of the organism, whose unity is merely the juxtaposition of extrinsic parts, whereas for Eisenstein the unity of the organism is first of all a unity of production: the organism produces its parts according to the laws of growth and genesis, just as the oppositions that threaten unity are not accidental but result from the internal force of the organism that shatters unity to reproduce it on a higher level. Eisenstein subscribes to the organic conception of montage that leads from a general situation to the modified situation by way of actions, but for him the organism is a *dialectical* unity: his assemblage [*agencement*] of movement-images must therefore follow very different rules.

Eisenstein himself gives a very elaborate theoretical presentation of these ideas in relation to *Battleship Potemkin* (1925), which he considers to be his first truly accomplished film.[4] He replaces parallel montage with a montage of opposition: instead of a simple juxtaposition of parts, the situation itself is divided along multiple lines of opposition. This opposition is *quantitative* (one man, several men; one ship, a fleet of ships; a single shot, a salvo), *qualitative* (sea, land), or *dynamic* (upward movement, downward movement, etc.). Such oppositions can be found at every level of the film—in the whole, in the different sequences, and in singular images themselves—because the dialectical law of the genesis and growth of the organism implies that any scission by opposition must be recomposed into a new unity of a higher degree. In the same way, Eisenstein substitutes convergent montage with montage by qualitative leaps—for example, the moment when a new consciousness is attained and a new quality surges up, when one passes from sadness to anger, or from resignation to revolt. For Eisenstein, this is the pathetic moment that is added to the moment of organic growth; what is designated is no longer the unity of opposites but the passage of one into the other and the creation of a new unity.

Finally, if Eisenstein, like Griffith, believes that time is an indirect image that flows from the organic composition of movement-images, he nonetheless has a different conception of both the interval and the whole. The interval becomes the power of the instant that attains the status of qualitative leap, while the whole as immensity or the open spiral of time no longer assembles a pregiven empirical reality from the outside but constitutes the very manner in which the dialectical reality is produced. "Things truly plunge *into* time," writes Deleuze: the forty-eight hours of the events of *Battleship Potemkin* or the ten days of *October* (1928) are major examples of the way Eisenstein conceives a time that can produce the dialectical life of the organism from within (*C1*, 37/57).

Whether "empirical" or dialectical, the whole of the film is given only in montage. There are as many different ways of conceiving of the whole as there are of assembling [*agencer*] movement-images; nonetheless, time does not have its own image: it is only presented indirectly, through the connection and comparison of movement-images. It is as if time were always hiding "behind" perceptions, affections, and actions, the only types of image that movement seems able to produce. It is as if Proust's desire for "a little time in its pure state" were entirely foreign to cinema. But Griffith and Eisenstein also agree on another important point. Montage always creates a connection between perception-images, affection-images, and action-images, although the equilibrium between the different types of image varies. Griffith and Eisenstein's organic montage is an active montage: perceptions and affects play a very important role but one that follows from the logic of actions. This is not necessarily the case in cinema: Vertov, according to Deleuze, invented a properly perceptive montage and thus became the spiritual father of all experimental cinema—something that Eisenstein, indeed, had already accused him of; just as Dreyer, with *The Passion of Joan of Arc* (1928) would later create an almost purely affective montage (*C1*, 70/103). If Griffith and Eisenstein privilege the active form of montage, it is because they share a faith in human agency and in history. However different their conceptions of history might be, they share the belief that history is made through humans' actions, and in this respect it matters little whether what triggers the events is the passions of a traitor, the love of a woman, or class struggle. The form of classic cinema—American cinema, doubtless, but not only American—is constructed around the action-image.

Deleuze calls this the *large form,* a term he borrows from Noël Burch. Burch used it to describe the structure of Fritz Lang's *M.* Deleuze makes it into the model of any film based on an organic structure that goes from the general situation to a modified situation by way of an action, according to the formula S-A-S' (*C1,* 142/197). Many different genres are constructed on the model of the large form of the action-image: westerns, documentaries, psychological or historical films, to which we will return. What they all have in common is that they are realist films, at least in Deleuze's sense of the term. For him, realism is in no way opposed to fiction or dream; it is perfectly able to integrate the extraordinary, the heroic, and the melodramatic, and its nature is not to present a simulacrum of everyday life. Rather, realism is defined through its conception of *milieus* and *behaviors.* Cinema has the ability to extract affects and qualities from determined people and places in order to show them as purely expressive, as we have already seen in the case of affects and as we will see in the next chapter in the case of spaces. Realism does exactly the opposite: it shows only "space-times" that are perfectly determined from a geographical, historical, and social perspective ("milieus") and affects that exist only when incarnated in behaviors. In his 1945 lecture "Cinema and the New Psychology," Merleau-Ponty described such a realistic tendency of cinema in terms of a "fundamental realism" shared by cinema and the modern novel along with the new philosophy and the new psychology.[5] This "fundamental realism" is in fact a form of behaviorism: feelings and thoughts no longer spring from a disincarnate spirit but are given in conducts, and there is no consciousness that is not bound to a body and thrown into a world where it coexists with others. Cinema gives us things and bodies to see and perceive, and it cannot count on any invisible interiority; it would thus by nature be "behaviorist." If these analyses of Merleau-Ponty do not exhaust cinema's essence, in Deleuze's view, they nevertheless provide an accurate description of an important aspect of realist cinema. They do not, however, place enough emphasis on another aspect that, for Deleuze, is still more decisive.

Cinematographic realism rests entirely on sensorimotor links, as described by Bergson, to which it adds an organic representation. In effect, it implies that characters are able to perceive the significant traits of a general situation—for instance, the signs of the hidden presence of Indians that often make westerns a drama of the visible and the invisible—in order to act in an adequate manner, to respond to the situation, and to modify it. In the same way, the organic conception structures the sensorimotor schema of action-perception into a series of terms that are simultaneously "correlative and antagonistic": situation and character, action as duel or series of duels (with the milieu, with others, with itself, etc.), the initial situation and the modified situation, and so on (*CI*, 142/197). The modified situation, moreover, need not necessarily be better, and the S-A-S′ form need not always narrate the story of a conquest or a victory. Sometimes, although less frequently, what is narrated is in fact a degradation. Certain examples of the American film noir, such as Hawks's *Scarface,* show the progressive decomposition of a hero battling with a pathogenic milieu, thus reviving the great literary tradition of Jack London or F. Scott Fitzgerald.[6] The healthy community, which believes in its values, in itself, and in its future,[7] is doubled with the pathogenic, criminal, or alcoholic community, which has lost all its hopes and illusions and sees life as a jungle. But the two communities cannot be opposed as dream-state and wakefulness. According to Deleuze, it is wrong to criticize "the American dream for being only a dream": on its confident side, it knows itself, and wants itself, to be a dream, to be an affirmation of vital illusions, "realist illusions which are more true than pure truth" (*CI*, 148/205). From this Deleuze concludes that, in a sense, American cinema never stopped refilming the same foundational film, the birth of a nation-civilization, of which Griffith gave the first example. American cinema, like Soviet cinema, believes in universal history and its finality. Of course, in the one case, it is a question of the dawning of the American nation and, in the other, of the advent of the proletariat. But is the difference really so great? Not according to Deleuze: Hollywood and the American dream are also a revolutionary dream. For Deleuze, the new world of immigrants and the new communist world are less opposed than one would like to believe—or than one would like to us believe.[8]

It is perhaps because history underlies all of American cinema that the genre of historical film strictly speaking was so important to Hollywood. This genre, which is all too easily or naively mocked, in fact plays out the most important aspects of the nineteenth-century conception of history. Deleuze invokes Nietzsche's second *Untimely Meditation*, "On the Uses and Disadvantages of History for Life," and the three characteristics of history he distinguishes: the monumental, the antiquarian, and the critical or ethical. All of these, claims Deleuze, can be found in historical films, which therefore give Nietzsche's analyses an unexpected topicality.[9] Without going into detail, it is important to note that all the traits of universal history converge and attain their meaning in relation to the last, which Deleuze calls an "ethical image" that evaluates universal history and organizes the value of actions:

> [I]t is a matter of Good and Evil, with all the temptations or the horrors of Evil (the barbarians, the unbelievers, the intolerant, the orgy, etc.). The ancient or recent past must submit to trial, go to course, in order to disclose what it is that produces decadence and what it is that produces new life. . . . A strong ethical judgement must condemn the injustice of "things," bring compassion, herald the new civilisation on the march, in short, constantly rediscover America . . . more especially as, from the beginning, all examination of causes has been dispensed with. The American cinema is content to illustrate the weakening of a civilisation in the milieu, and the intervention of a traitor in the action. But the marvel is that, with all these limits, it has succeeded in putting forward a strong and coherent conception of universal history, monumental, antiquarian and ethical. (*C1*, 151/209)

Montage, the operation that produces the Whole and makes the indirect presentation of time follow from the assemblage [*agencement*] of movement-images, is not necessarily organic; nevertheless, organico-active montage became the dominant model of prewar cinema". The "universal triumph" of American cinema, with contributions from many foreign filmmakers, was constituted around the sensorimotor schema, around the centrality of the action-image and its attendant realism. It is no surprise that the realist cinema of the action-image is closely related to a belief in history and its finality. Actions are human actions, and if humans can understand a general situation and respond to it adequately, if they can defy wickedness and stupidity, one can keep hoping that someday, sooner or later, universal history will attain its end, that America will finally be the land of all immigrants just as the Soviet Union will be the land of all proletarians, and that the new person will achieve his or her spiritual regeneration.

Deleuze's remarks are neither cynical nor derisory. As we will see, he himself will espouse the necessity of belief.[10] But he sees this conception of universal and ethical history as a nineteenth-century idea. It is strange that cinema—the twentieth-century art par excellence, an art that is new beyond any doubt, in Deleuze's eyes—would take up the conceptions of an outdated history and that it would do so through its most distinctive and innovative technique: the assemblage of movement-images. As Deleuze does not explicitly take up this issue, I suggest the following hypothesis. The twentieth century begins only after the war. It is the rise of Fascism, Nazism, Stalinism, and World War II that destroys the faith in history. The complicity and alliance of certain arts and of a certain cinema—and not necessarily mediocre cinema—with the worst kind of politics does not help matters (*C2*, 164ff/213ff). The hopes confided in cinema and in its power of creating a new thought and transforming the world "ring [strangely] today": "we put them to one side like declarations worthy of a museum," writes Deleuze (*C2*, 164/213). What is certain, in any case, is that the action-image comes into crisis. It is undone by the rise of other signs and other images. And *in place of history*, it is *time itself* that breaks through directly in the image.

4 Postwar Cinema

Time appears when it is felt, beyond events, as the
weight of truth.

Andrei Tarkovsky, *Sculpting in Time*

"[T]he signs of play and the signs of death may be the same on a child's face, at least for those of us who cannot penetrate its mystery," wrote André Bazin in 1949, regarding Rossellini's *Germany Year Zero*.[1] The child, Edmund, has just assassinated his sickly and self-admittedly "useless" father, an act that we know to have been triggered by the speech of a Nazi schoolmaster. But we know nothing about the child's reasons for the murder, since all we can read in his face is an attentive concentration; we can draw no conclusions about his feelings, nor can we decide between indifference, pain, or cruelty: this is the child's business and his secret. In the endless walk that follows, Rossellini's poetics asserts itself even more clearly. The child walks among ruins, people and things abandon him, and we see his "pensive" face without knowing what is on his mind. It is only after the fact, after Edmund throws himself from the top of the bombed-out building, that we finally understand.

This description of *Germany Year Zero* (1947) encapsulates Bazin's whole reading of Rossellini's cinema and, more generally, the characteristics that he attributes to postwar Italian neorealism. Definitions of *neorealism* that are restricted to the topicality of scenarios, the use of nonprofessional actors, location shooting, social content, etc., are very reductive. They fail to take the form of these films into account, and they thus forget that in cinema, as in all art, realism is an *aesthetic* that is chosen and defined by formal criteria rather than a pure and simple erasure of style in the face of raw reality. What Bazin foregrounds in Rossellini's work is the profound coherence of a choice that is simultaneously ethical and aesthetic. Because reality is enigmatic, complex, and fragmentary, because its meaning is never given on the surface of things but must always be deciphered by the spirit, Rossellini never imposes a preestablished meaning of images on his spectators. This implies a precise aesthetic choice, an inversion of the shot's subordination to montage. We cannot dwell here on Bazin's famous analyses, but we should remember that he criticized certain techniques of montage for producing a logical cutting of reality and a linkage between images such that the meaning of the film was preestablished in relation to the images themselves, a meaning given beyond the images by montage alone.[2] By privileging the shot, and in particular the sequence shot, it was possible to restore a fragmented, incomplete, and never preestablished meaning to reality and to leave the task of active interpretation to the spectators. This is why Bazin ended his critique of *Germany Year Zero* with a tribute to Rossellini that is simultaneously a veritable profession of faith:

> We are not moved by the actor or the event, but by the meaning we are forced to extract from them. In this *mise en scène,* the moral or dramatic significance is never visible on the surface of reality; nevertheless we can't fail to sense what that significance is if we have a consciousness. Isn't this, then, a sound definition of realism in art: to force the mind to take sides on beings and things without cheating?[3]

It should be added that this profession of faith depends on a *cinema of time,* a point that will be very important for Deleuze. What Bazin admires in both Italian neorealism and Orson Welles, despite their immense differences, is, of course, their relative marginalization of montage. But this is merely the negative side of a positive phenomenon: depth shots and sequence shots are opposed to montage because, rather than playing "tricks with time and space," they offer us "condensing time" in which events and beings retain their depth.[4]

The child in *Germany Year Zero* is not the only Rossellini character to walk in a city that has lost its reassuringly realist aspect, a city whose spaces have lost their recognizable function. In *Europe 51* (1952), an upper-middle-class woman walks through her city, but she can no longer relate what she sees to her everyday preoccupations, finally stopping short in front of a factory without recognizing it. But what does "not recognizing" mean in this context? Is it a simple failure of memory, recognition, or reason—at her family's request, the woman will be locked up in a psychiatric hospital—or is it a new experience of the mind? Deleuze describes the situation as follows:

> Her glances relinquish the practical function of a mistress of a house who arranges things and beings, and pass through every state of an internal vision, affliction, compassion, love, happiness, acceptance, extending to the psychiatric hospital where she is locked up at the end of a new trial of Joan of Arc: she sees, she has learnt to see. (*C2*, 2/8–9)

The woman who no longer "recognizes" a factory nonetheless sees it; she can see it all the better because she does not "recognize" it. Learning to see, or in any case making seeing the central experience, is, for Deleuze, the distinctive discovery of neorealism, which is a cinema of the seer in the strict sense of the word. Even as he recognizes the richness of Bazin's theses and their superiority to content-based interpretations, Deleuze expresses some reservations and proposes another thesis: the change that neorealism introduced with its new type of cinematographic images should be understood not on the level of reality but on the level of the mental and of thought. But what exactly is the scope of Deleuze's disagreement with Bazin, and what does he mean by this apparent opposition between the real and the mental?

The first reason why Deleuze cannot subscribe to Bazin's thesis—that neorealism is more faithful to the enigmatic and fragmentary nature of the real—is that, despite itself, it reintroduces the ontological reduplication of the thing and the representation of the thing that Deleuze, following Bergson, wants to combat at any price. The second reason engages a more complex relation to Bazin: if neorealism should be analyzed on the level of thought and mind rather than the real, this is because the "mental" opens onto previously unexplored dimensions of time. This new cinema produces direct images of time, true time-images beyond movement. And this is where Deleuze in his own way takes up the legacy of Bazin, who saw time as the vocation proper to a cinema that can give us not only the image of things, but also "the image of their duration, change mummified as it were."[5] Understanding what such direct time-images are will require additional analyses.

What does Deleuze mean by "cinema of the seer"? In the first place, he means a cinema that breaks the sensorimotor links that connected the material levels of subjectivity and divided movement-images into perceptions, actions, and affections. If we remember that for Bergson perceiving involves subtracting everything that does not interest us from the thing, or, in other words, perceiving means recognizing what is useful to us in things from the point of view of action, we are in a better position to understand why Deleuze claims that the less we recognize, the better we see.[6] The heroine of *Europe 51* no longer recognizes the factory because she has become unable or unwilling to make use of it, to situate it in the margins of her world as the necessary site of work or of exploitation, as any point of reference whatever in the city's geography. What is broken is the force of habit that allows things and beings to be recognized so long as they are confined to their assigned places and functions. But precisely when this recognition fails, one can see through the clichés that structure our "natural" and social habits of perception. Or, as Bazin puts it in a different context: "Only the impassive lens, stripping its object of all those ways of seeing it, those piled-up preconceptions, that spiritual dust and grime with which my eyes have covered it, is able to present it in all its virginal purity to my attention and consequently to my love."[7]

Rather than being linked to action, perception ceaselessly returns to the object.[8] It thus loses the pragmatic function of preparing an adequate response to the milieu and the situation. In effect, according to Deleuze, the characters in films by Rossellini, Visconti, Fellini, or Antonioni do not act, or at least not in the sense of realist cinema, which established the links between movement-images through sensorimotor schema. In the old mode of realism, Deleuze writes, characters were reacting to situations even when they were bound and gagged; now, even when they are running and moving they no longer have any hold on the world that surrounds them, the world that makes them "see and hear what is no longer subject to the rules of a response or an action" (*C2*, 3/9). In the place of sensorimotor links, other links between images appear; action-images and even movement-images tend to disappear or in any case become subordinate to what Deleuze calls "purely optical [and] sound [situations]," the "build-up" of which is what defines neorealism strictly speaking (*C2*, 2/9).[9]

What do these purely optical and sound situations produce, if they are no longer prolonged into action? They are not simply affection-images; they do not fill the gap between a perception that recognizes and an action that responds: if they are *pure*, it is because they only give something to be seen and heard. But what, exactly? For Bergson, sensorimotor perception is in the service of the—legitimate—needs of the living, but Deleuze is less concerned in this context with the demands of life than with a system of values that clings to the very perception of things, always at risk of letting thought slip into the conformism of the *doxa* and letting affects slip into preestablished patterns.[10] Because, however violent sensorimotor situations might be, everything becomes tolerable when it is caught in a system of actions and reactions:

> We see, and we more or less experience, a powerful organization of poverty and oppression. And we are precisely not without sensory-motor schemata for recognizing such things, for putting up with and approving of them and for behaving ourselves subsequently, taking into account our situation, our capabilities, and our taste. We have schemata for turning away when it is too unpleasant,

for prompting resignation when it is terrible and for assimilating when it is too beautiful. (*C2*, 20/31–32)

Purely optical and sound situations, to the contrary, surge up when links between actions are undone and when we, along with the character, are abandoned to what there is to see, to that which is too beautiful or too unbearable, not only in extreme situations but also in the smallest fragments of everyday life. This cinema of becoming-visionary produces images in which the critique of the order of things as it is, is inseparable from an act of compassion, interest, or love for things and beings, a way of warning us against forms of cynicism whose critical power is illusory (*C2*, 19/30). The action-image is undone along multiple lines of fracture. We have already seen that the sensorimotor link is broken or distended to the point that responses are no longer pragmatically regulated, at the same time as the global situation gives way to a dispersive reality in which events are no longer connected to each other by a "line of the universe." The links between characters and between events are weakened, governed by no other necessity than chance encounters. Space itself is affected: well-defined and recognizable places disappear in favor of what Deleuze calls "disconnected" spaces and "any-space-whatevers" that are no longer the appropriate setting for an action or for a determined situation.[11] Postwar cities, demolished or in the midst of reconstruction, provide such spaces in themselves, but their appearance is not contingent, and they will not disappear with the traces of the war. Certain directors make them a central element in their films: in *The Eclipse* (1961), Antonioni makes characters and events disappear, leaving a more and more empty space on the screen.

But what happened such that cinema changed in this way? Why, after the war, did tendencies that were always present, if isolated, in cinema rush headlong toward an irreversible crisis of the action-image and the emergence of a new type of image? For Deleuze, there is no doubt that what happened to cinema cannot be undone. He knows, of course, that all kinds of action films are still being made and will continue to be made, but "the soul of cinema no longer [takes that route]" (*C1*, 206/278). What happened to cinema includes many things of different natures, but they all converge toward the same result. There were causes internal to art and, in particular, to literature and cinema,[12] but there were also social, political, and moral causes. The war and its aftermath shook the American dream, and cinema's power as mass art showed a sinister face as an instrument of propaganda at the service of the worst powers (*C2*, 164/214). Not to mention the inflation of images "in the external world and in people's heads" (*C1*, 206/278). It is a commonplace to say that we live in a civilization of the image, but, according to Deleuze, it would be much more precise to call it a civilization of the *cliché*, by which he means a "sensorimotor image of the thing" in the strictly Bergsonian sense: never the whole image, always a little less, and only that which interests us. Whence the vital necessity and difficult struggle for cinema to produce images that are not clichés or that do not become clichés again too quickly. This is how Deleuze understands Godard's famous demand, "No just images, just an image [pas d'images justes, juste une image]"; if one were capable of creating an image, the image alone would be enough to restore the thing in itself, in "its excess of beauty or horror," and it would thus liberate a seeing whose power is still unknown to us. Pure optical and sound images alone do not necessarily guarantee us such a power. In order to undo the action-image, such images often seem to depend on arrested movement and to rediscover the cinematographic force of the static shot: the still-lives in Ozu's films or Antonioni's obsessive framing[13] and empty spaces are among the best examples of this. If these images are not a new, different kind of cliché, however, it is because they are not limited to disturbing sensorimotor links; on the contrary, they are capable of creating other links with different forces, forces of time and of thought, that open images to other dimensions "beyond movement" (*C2*, 20ff/32ff). The subsequent chapter will clarify what Deleuze means by connections of images that explore time and thought "beyond movement," by a cinema of time that turns itself toward the spiritual dimension of subjectivity. But first, one more important point in the postwar crisis must be analyzed.

How is it possible that organic montage—the mode of assemblage [*agencement*] of movement-images that, in Deleuze's own eyes, had made "classic" cinema great—would not only fall into crisis but would become the paradigm of moral and aesthetic bankruptcy? In other words, how did it come about that sensorimotor links and the action-image lost their force of conviction, and why did they become "clichés"? If not explicitly formulated by Deleuze, this question is nonetheless in the backdrop of his analyses of the shift from "classic" to "modern" cinema. And his answer is fairly easy to make explicit. For Griffith, Eisenstein, and many others, the grandeur of organic representation was sustained by faith in human, individual, and collective action—which is to say by faith in history, as we have seen. The war—a name that stands here for the whole constellation of events that preceded, accompanied, and followed it—tore apart confidence in human action: we no longer believe that an action can have bearing on a global situation or unveil its meaning even in part; we no longer believe in a human becoming of the world. The "healthiest" and most necessary illusions begin to fail us. Then, and only then, what had given classic cinema its greatness and honor can be repeated only as a hollow form. Then, and only then, sensorimotor schemata become clichés in cinema as in life. The less we believe in these schemata, the more we use them. Henceforward, according to Deleuze, cinema will look elsewhere:

> The soul of cinema demands increasing thought, even if thought begins by undoing the system of actions, perceptions and affections on which the cinema had fed up to that point. (*C1*, 206/278)

The terms *time, thought,* and even *spirit* keep returning in characterizing the change that intervened in cinematographic images. They will be analyzed in the next chapter, but even here we should make one thing clear: Deleuze does not subscribe to any dualism whatever; he does not reintroduce a form of transcendence as an answer to our failing hopes in the progress of human history; quite the opposite. The thought and spirit that cinema needs (and that we, too, need) are immanent powers of life, which hold the hope and pose the challenge of creating new links between humans and *this* world.[14]

Scholars have often noted a "contradiction" between Deleuze's project as he initially describes it—in the first lines of the foreword to *Cinema 1* he declares, "This study is not a history of the cinema. It is a taxonomy, an attempt at the classification of images and signs"—and the role of caesura that he goes on to ascribe to the postwar period.[15] Indeed, it does seem that a historical event provokes the dramatic swing from the regime of the movement-image to that of the time-image and that this historical event thus powerfully intervenes as a principle of classification in a study that claims to be a "natural history of images." Seeking out "contradictions" is not necessarily the best methodology for a history of philosophy in general, and, in this specific case, the tension is so obvious that it would be hard, even for Deleuze, not to notice it. I would like to suggest that what seems on first reading to be a blunt contradiction is instead a perfectly consistent, powerful, and challenging philosophical claim on Deleuze's part, although a counterintuitive one. As we have seen, Deleuze responds to the jibes hastily aimed at Hollywood's conception of history by invoking Nietzsche and retorting that Hollywood in fact had a powerful and coherent vision of History: that of the nineteenth century. Along with the sensorimotor links and the pragmatic patterns of perception, the Second World War also shakes, first and foremost, this concept of universal history that was profoundly dependent on a pragmatic, "realistic" notion of human agency. For Deleuze, who was always overtly suspicious of historical categories, this amounts to saying that what is definitively in crisis is the concept of History itself. There will be no history of the twentieth century, certainly not in the Hegelian sense of a supposed end of history: every discourse that announces the end of history, philosophy, modernity, or anything else is profoundly foreign to Deleuze's thought.[16] There will be no history of the twentieth century in the sense that the twentieth century begins after the war, precisely when old conceptions of history give way to other temporal concepts such as becoming and the event.[17] Indeed, the very project of a classification of images in the sense of natural history is made possible, for Deleuze, by the crisis of the action-image and the emergence of a cinema of time. It is because notions of universal history are no longer available to us, have lost their power of conviction, that Deleuze's taxonomy of images becomes thinkable. Time presents itself as such where history fades away.

5 ▌ *The Time-Image*

> *But at least, if strength were granted me for long*
> *enough to accomplish my work, I should not fail, even*
> *if the results were to make them resemble monsters, to*
> *describe men first and foremost as occupying a place,*
> *a very considerable place compared with the restricted*
> *one which is allotted to them in space, a place on the*
> *contrary prolonged past measure—for simultaneously,*
> *like giants plunged into the years, they touch epochs that*
> *are immensely far apart, separated by the slow accretion*
> *of many, many days—in Time.*
>
> Marcel Proust, *Time Regained*

For time to present itself in person in cinema, the most certain appearance must be shaken: the image is not always in the present. Because of the presupposition that movement-images are in the present, montage was given the function of composing the indirect image of time and of expressing on its own the "whole that changes" of the film. The different practices and theories of montage are always strictly related to certain conceptions of time. Eisenstein explained that montage could not limit itself to being a simple juxtaposition of parts because time is not the juxtaposition of instants. And Pasolini granted montage the power to achieve time by making "the present past," just as "death achieves a dazzling montage of our life."[1] Yet movement-images and shots must already have a temporal character, or it is not clear how their synthesis could produce the image of the whole. Classic reflection on cinema thus turns, according to Deleuze, on this alternative between montage and shot. Philosophy had encountered a similar problem when it thought of time as "the number of movement"; either the number is an independent instance, or else it depends on what it measures. This, however, is not a real alternative but rather two sides of the same indirect representation of time, which Deleuze summarizes as follows: "[T]ime depends on movement, but through the intermediary of montage; it flows from montage, but as if subordinate to movement" (*C2, 36/52*).

In short, the alternative between shot and montage, continually reopened in cinematographic theory, depends on the presupposition that images are in the present, which, in turn, presupposes a conception of time as measure of movement. But for movement to subordinate time as its measure, movement itself must be normal. By "normal" movement, Deleuze means any movement that can be related to a center. A center of revolution, a center of observation for a spectator, or a center of gravity for moving bodies: the possibility of being centered is what makes movement measurable, because subject to relations of number, and therefore "normal." At the same time, an acentered movement is no longer subject to measurement and becomes "abnormal" or "aberrant." Far from breaking time, such a movement, according to Deleuze, frees time from subordination and gives it the chance to surface directly. It follows that a direct presentation of time does not need to stop or fix the image, which would be very difficult in cinema, an art of moving images, but rather that this direct presentation is one with aberrant movement (*C2, 34ff/50ff*).

Now for Deleuze, as we have seen, the movement-image itself is by nature an acentered, aberrant movement. Epstein had already noted all the abnormalities of movement that confronted spectators: a man may run as far as possible, but he always stays in front of us; movements are inverted, accelerated and decelerated, changed in scale, etc.[2] What emerges in such movements that cannot be reduced to our motor experiences is a *perception* of time:

> What aberrant movement reveals is time as the Whole, as "infinite opening," as anteriority over all normal movement defined by motivity [*motricité*]: time has to be anterior to the controlled flow of every action. . . . If normal movement subordinates the time of which it gives us an indirect representation, aberrant movement

speaks up for an anteriority of time that it presents to us directly, on the basis of the disproportion of scales, the dissipation of centres and the false continuity of the images themselves. (*C2*, 37/54; translation modified)

Not only is the image never in the present, but it always has a temporal density: it is possessed by a past and a future that haunt it and that in no way coincide with the actual images that precede and follow it. The image thus has a "before" and an "after" that coexist with its present. Moreover, the present itself is often merely the elusive limit of an image that swings between past and future, as in one of the famous sequences of Orson Welles's *Citizen Kane* (1941), where Kane walks toward his journalist friend to complete the break with him and is moving, according to Deleuze, not through space but time. It is a truly Proustian cinema, in which beings occupy a place in time that is incommensurable with the place they hold in space.[3] If this is the case, it is because time cannot be reduced to its chronological dimension, in which one instant follows another. Abnormal movement cannot even superficially be correlated with space covered, and as it makes visible a pure movement extracted from the moving body [*mobile*], it also frees the possibility for time to be perceived directly, without letting it be reduced to the trajectory of a moving body. On Deleuze's reading, Bergson's desire to extract from movement "the mobility that is its essence" is strictly united with Proust's desire to attain "a little time in its pure state." Cinema, which was able to restore purity to movement since it began, has also always been able to present time. What changes from "classic cinema" to "modern cinema" is that time becomes an explicit issue, and new ways of connecting images are created.[4] As organic representation is undone, the *crystalline image* replaces it.

We have seen how Deleuze characterizes purely optical and sound images, but we have not yet analyzed the other types of images to which they are linked, the new links that replace a weakened sensorimotor perception. Here Bergson intervenes once again: the cinema's "Bergsonism" is not limited to the movement-image but also concerns the time-image in decisive ways.[5] In the second chapter of *Matter and Memory*, Bergson distinguishes two different forms of intellectual effort: habitual or automatic perception and attentive perception.[6] The first form of perception, which we have already encountered, is prolonged in movements structured by habits, a recognition that takes place in us without requiring any effort other than repetition. "[T]he cow recognizes grass, I recognize my friend Peter," writes Deleuze, and as "the cow moves from one clump of grass to another, . . . with my friend Peter, I move from one subject of conversation to another."[7] This is because habitual perception follows a horizontal movement: one passes from one object to another, always remaining on the same plane. For Bergson, however, attentive perception functions in a very different way, and only an associationist conception of the psyche could maintain that new elements are added to old ones without requiring a transformation of the system as a whole. In the second kind of perception, one does not remain on the same horizontal plane, and one does not slip from one object to another; rather, perception never stops returning to the object, thus forming a *circuit* with it. The unity between the act of mind and the perceived object is such that each time attention or concentration deepens, it forms a new, wider circuit that envelops the first but that shares with it only the perceived object. In fact the intimate relation between the act of the mind and the perceived object extends further still, since it is a matter more precisely of a double system of circuits that correspond to each other, circuits of memory and circuits of reality, for which Bergson gives a famous schema (see Figure 1).

Circle A contains only the object and is the closest to an immediate perception that nonetheless is not pure because memory, according to Bergson, always mixes in with perception. Circles B, C, and D represent the widening degrees of memory that correspond, respectively, to circles B′, C′, and D′, which represent deeper and deeper strata of the object. Attentive perception, ceaselessly returning to the object, thus provokes the simultaneous expansion of memory *and* of knowledge of reality, of matter *and* of spirit:

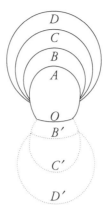

Figure 1.

> [I]t will be seen that the progress of attention results in creating anew not only the object perceived, but also the ever widening systems with which it may be bound up; so that in the measure in which the circles B, C, D represent a higher expansion of memory, their reflection attains in B′, C′, D′ deeper strata of reality. (*MM*, 105/115)

Translated into terms of cinema, this proposition presents us with two different sorts of images: sensorimotor images, on the one hand, and optical and sound images, on the other. For Deleuze, the first are only apparently richer and more concrete. They are extended into movement and seem to give us the thing itself insofar as we can use it. But, insofar as it is useful, the "thing itself" loses all specificity and is merely an abstraction: after all, the cow is interested in grass in general, not in this tuft of grass in particular. On the other hand, optical and sound images—which initially seem to be abstract and "subjective," insofar as they seem to confront us with descriptions, with points of view on the thing rather than with the thing itself— prove to be much richer. Deleuze here establishes a close connection between Bergson's theory of attentive perception and the theory of descriptions that Alain Robbe-Grillet places at the center of the poetics of the *nouveau-roman*.[8] For Robbe-Grillet, description should aspire to "erase" the concrete object, to efface it so as to retain only a few singular traits, even if this means adding other descriptions to the first in order to foreground different aspects of the object, in an open process in which every description is provisional and replaceable but also absolutely singular. And it is precisely this singularity that gives the optical image its richness: it retains only one aspect, sometimes a simple line or point, but in this way it brings the thing to an "essential singularity" (*C2*, 45/64). The complicity between the *nouveau roman* and the *nouvelle vague* is well known. Not only did Robbe-Grillet, himself a filmmaker, cosign with Alain Resnais one of the manifesto films of the new French cinema, *Last Year in Marienbad* (1961), but the technique of description-shots played an important role in Jean-Luc Godard's method (*C2*, 45/63).

Rossellini had already given a striking cinematic example of a single object able to pass through ever-widening circuits that deepened the knowledge of the object as much as they deepened explorations of thought. In *Stromboli, terra di Dio* (1950), the island is described in expanding circuits: the approaches to the island, the tuna fishing, the storm, etc., which culminate with the eruption of the volcano. At the same time, the foreign woman passes through ever-deeper circuits of thought and spiritual experience:

> There are no longer sensory-motor images with their extensions, but much more complex circular links between pure optical and sound images, on the one hand, and on the other hand images from time and thought, on planes which all coexist by right, constituting the soul and body of the island. (*C2*, 47/66)

Each circuit is independent in principle and always creates a new image, or a new description of the object; it can thus join or contradict the other circuits. Nonetheless, according to Deleuze, the intended object is always the same, and the set of circuits will constitute "the layers of one and the same physical reality, and the levels of one and the same mental reality, memory or spirit" (*C2*, 46/65). The optical and sound image, the description of the object, no longer answers to action but rather calls on another dimension of images and of subjectivity: the *actual* optical image is linked to a *virtual* image, and together they form a circuit.[9] In the universe of movement-images, as we saw, subjectivity surges as what distends matter and introduces a gap between a received movement and an executed movement, between an action and a reaction. Affection itself belongs to this first moment of subjectivity because it also subsists on the gap in matter, the gap between perception and action, which it occupies without filling. The first level of subjectivity is thus literally material because it is nothing but distended, quartered matter, the interval of movement. But here, with the virtual images that come from time and thought, we are faced with another dimension of subjectivity that is not opposed to the first, but opens up on another perspective:

> It makes full use of the gap, it assumes it, because it lodges itself there, but it is of a different nature. Subjectivity, then, takes on a new sense, which is no longer motor or material, but temporal and spiritual: that which "is added" to matter, not what distends it. (*C2*, 47/67)

This new mental or spiritual dimension of subjectivity is no more an autonomous instance than its material counterpart. The living image, as we have seen in detail, has no ascendancy over other images; it is held on the same plane of immanence, which allows Bergson, and later Deleuze, to say that we perceive *in* things and that conscious perception is in no way a mirror that reflects and reduplicates the world. Likewise, memory and thought are not only psychological realities "inside" our minds, or brains: they exist, or insist, in time; it is not time that is in us, but we who are in time. Let us now turn our attention to the ontological nature of time.

In effect, if optical and sound images are linked with recollection-images, dream-images, or world-images in widening circuits, the latter assume as their condition of possibility the smallest and most internal circuit, the "extreme point" where the actual image is contracted in the encounter with its own virtual image (*C2*, 68/92). Together they crystallize, giving us the key to other circuits that are revealed to be slivers of the crystal-image, "crystals of time." For there to be a crystal-image, the actual and the virtual must become indiscernible, and the two sides of the image must become unattributable, without their distinction being called into question. The mirror is a classic means of producing crystal-images in which the actual and the virtual trade places. Welles's *Lady from Shanghai* offers a famous example in the scene in the palace of mirrors: the omnipresence of mirrors makes virtual images proliferate to the point that they seem to have absorbed the whole actuality of the character, who becomes one "virtuality" among others. For Deleuze, this is a crystal-image in its pure state because the actual and the virtual, without being confused, have nonetheless become indiscernible. The only way that the two characters can win back their actuality is to smash all the mirrors; then they can find each other (and kill each other) (*C2*, 70/95).

But what exactly is a virtual image? And what is signified by its coalescence with the actual image in the crystal? Deleuze credits Bergson with constantly posing this question and seeking its answer in "time's abyss" (*C2*, 78/105). The actual is easy to define, since it has only one temporal mode: the present. Everything that is present is actual and vice versa. But according to Bergson, the status of the present itself is less simple than it seems: we always say that the present changes or passes, that it becomes the past when a new present replaces it, without seeing that herein lies the problem and that the foundation of becoming-past as such is what must be understood. Bergson's answer is apparently paradoxical: the present passes because the past does not come after the present but is contemporaneous with it. Rather than imagining a present that would be gradually pushed into the past by the "coming" of a subsequent present, or even, in Husserl's sense, an "extended now" that would in itself have a double orientation toward the past and the future,[10] Bergson postulates the pure coexistence of the present and *its own* past. The present does not withdraw of itself, and the past need not wait to follow it: they are strictly contemporaneous. What separates and distinguishes them is not a temporal axis but the different modalities of the actual and the virtual: the present is actual, whereas its contemporaneous past is virtual.[11] The present is thus doubled with the memory of the present, and, for Bergson, their coexistence is revealed to be the real foundation of becoming-past. It explains why the present passes, why it gives way to a subsequent present: for Bergson, at least, just as movement cannot be made of immobilities, the past cannot be "made" with the present.

If Deleuze speaks in this context of a present that is an actual image and a past that is a virtual image, it is not unjustified in relation to *Matter and Memory,* where this splitting of time corresponds to that between actual perception and virtual memory. Bergson calls the virtual image of the present a "pure memory" to distinguish it from mental images, dreams, or recollections, with which it should not be confused. Such mental images are indeed virtual images, but they have become actualized, and necessarily actualized in relation to a present that is different from the present they had been. Pure memory, on the other hand, is the virtual image that is formed with its own actual image, its own present, the shortest circuit, the crystal that shows the genesis of time. If the presupposition that cinematographic images are always in the present is false, according to Deleuze, this is because the present image itself is doubled with its pure past:

> What constitutes the crystal-image is the most fundamental operation of time. . . . Time has to split at the same time as it sets itself out or unrolls itself: it splits in two dissymmetrical jets, one of which makes all the present pass on, while the other preserves all the past. Time consists of this split, and it is this, it is time, that we *see in the crystal.* . . . We see in the crystal the perpetual foundation of time, non-chronological time, Cronos and not Chronos. This is the powerful, non-organic Life which grips the world. (*C2,* 81/108–9)

The coexistence of present and past is not the only paradoxical thesis on time that Bergson defends; a second thesis completes it. The present passes, but the past itself does not pass: it is conserved in itself, endowed with its own virtual reality distinct from any psychological existence. To represent this conception of time, Bergson provides another famous schema, that of the inverted cone (see Figure 2 [from *MM,* 162/181]).

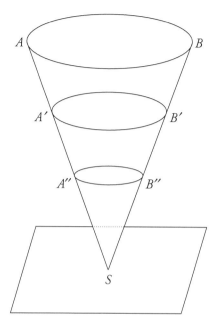

Figure 2.

Point S is the actual present, even if, as Deleuze remarks, it is not a point in the strict sense of the term, since it is already doubled with the virtual image of its past. The sections of the cone AB, A′B′, A″B″, etc., are virtual circuits, each of which constitutes the whole of our past in different degrees of contraction. But "our" past is not, according to Bergson, a psychological state: our memory as a faculty of the soul does not constitute the past, but rather it is *in the pure past* that we can create a memory for ourselves. We must place ourselves in the past as such in order to seek our recollections, and only the past in itself can give recollection-images the temporal depth that distinguishes them from dream-images or other mental images:

> The virtual image (pure memory) is not a psychological state or a consciousness: it exists outside of consciousness, in time, and we should have no more difficulty in admitting the virtual insistence

of pure memories in time than we do for the actual existence of non-perceived objects in space. . . . Just as we perceive things in the place where they are, and have to place ourselves among things in order to perceive them, we go to look for recollection in the place where it is, we have to place ourselves with a leap into the past in general, into these purely virtual images which have been constantly preserved through time. (*C2*, 80/107; translation modified)

The new sense of subjectivity, temporal or spiritual, that was encountered at the beginning of this chapter here acquires all its philosophical consistency. Deleuze is not in the least giving credence to some kind of vague spiritualism, nor is he reintroducing a form of transcendence. The new dimension that is added to the different aspects of material subjectivity is the subjectivity of time itself. In his early philosophy Bergson had identified duration with our interior life,[12] but he later reversed his perspective. Duration is no longer conceived as a psychological category but as an ontological field in itself. Time is not "in" the soul, nor is it an a priori form of the transcendental subject, as Kant maintained. Nonchronological time, time grasped in its foundation, is subjectivity itself—the only subjectivity, for Deleuze if not for Bergson. Time is what constitutes the interiority in which we live and change, allowing Deleuze to conclude, "Subjectivity is never ours, it is time, that is, the soul or the spirit, the virtual" (*C2*, 83/111).

Deleuze's formula, "cinema is Bergsonian" thus acquires its whole meaning (*C2*, 109/143). Cinema is Bergsonian insofar as it is an assemblage of movement-images and even more so as an assemblage of time-images. The exploration of the nonchronological dimension of time became the vocation of cinema, of a cinema that demands more and more thought (*C1*, 206/278). Orson Welles's *Citizen Kane* is, for Deleuze as for Bazin, the first great film of a cinema of time. The depth of field is not a simple technical asset: it has an aesthetic and ontological function, serving each time to explore a region of the past, a "sheet of the past." The succession of cross-cutting shot-reaction shots describes Kane's habits, the "dead time" of his life, while the depth shots mark moments in which Kane's life changes dramatically. At these points, the image operates, according to Deleuze, as a true leap into the past as such:

> The hero acts, walks and moves; but it is in the past that he plunges himself into and moves in: time is no longer subordinated to movement, but movement to time. Hence in the great scene where Kane catches up in depth with the friend he will break with, it is in the past that he himself moves; this movement *was* the break with the friend. (*C2*, 106/139)

Welles is not of course the only filmmaker of time, just as the exploration of sheets of the past, of layers of ontological memory, is not the only path the time-image can take. Filmmakers such as Resnais, Antonioni, Ozu, Godard, or Tarkovsky—by no means an exhaustive list—have each followed their own path and given time-images different forms. Even a schematic analysis of these works exceeds the scope of this study, but within our own limits, we have one last question to pose before concluding:

What happened to all of cinema's revolutionary hopes? What happened to its faith in the transformation of the world and of humans? Was that hope also broken, like the thread linking humans' actions to the world and to the universe? Time that surges and shows itself in person—what face does it show us, us humans?

6 ∎ *Images and Immanence*

The Problem of the World

It is when history is broken that time presents itself in its *pure state* and deploys all the power of its nonchronological dimensions. Deleuze, of course, always aimed at thinking and producing the concepts of a time that would not be subordinate to simple succession and still less to the teleological and dialectic grids that absorb every temporal event into history.[1] But his encounter with cinema obliged him to pose the problem of the disjunction of time and history while explicitly taking into account a broader configuration. For time to be *thinkable* and *livable* (for us), it is not enough that it present itself in person. By means of cinema, time becomes thinkable and livable, but in the process it acquires unexpected allies: belief, immanent conversion of faith, and (nondogmatic) images of thought.

For if, according to Deleuze, it is easy to do without the category of history, it is harder to dispense with everything that history gathered together and allowed to be thought coherently. The rise of time-images in postwar cinema takes on its value, in Deleuze's eyes, precisely because it is not limited to undoing the models of classic cinema. The ironic repetition of its clichés, attacks on and parodies of classic cinema, quickly reach their limits (*C1*, 210/284). And even aesthetic criteria are not enough to understand the importance of new cinema: modern films are neither more nor less beautiful than classic films, and the reason for the importance that Deleuze grants them must be sought elsewhere. The greatness of the filmmakers of time is that they were able to create other *livable* configurations of thought in images themselves; this is how they attained a force comparable to the now failing force of the action-image.[2] The force of organic representation derived from the properly cinematographic form that it was able to give to "the most necessary illusions of life." The relations of humans to each other and to the milieu, world, or universe were organized around action. These relations were not necessarily happy, and were sometimes even tragic, but they were nonetheless always inscribed within a horizon of possible meaning. The sensorimotor schema, the link between perception and action— which for Bergson was characteristic of all living formations, even the simplest—guaranteed humans a possible grasp on the situations and events that concerned them: the world, ordered or disordered, then made sense. From this perspective, failure and success were secondary; something like truth and falsity are secondary in relation to a meaning that precedes them and arranges their space of possibility (Deleuze, *Difference and Repetition*, 145ff/189ff).

But this is not everything. Most often, the link between humans was thought in a very specific form, that of a *people*, just as the link between peoples in the world was thought in the form of radical transformation: *revolution.* "Classic" cinema simultaneously constitutes and participates in the revolutionary dream of peoples. Eisenstein believed in the cinema of the "punch," in the violence of images able to create a shock in thought and thus awaken it to itself (*C2*, 156–57/203–4). As for Vertov, he gave the cine-eye the task of carrying perception in matter in order to "reconcile a non-human perception with the overman of the future, material community and formal communism" (*C1*, 83/121). These hopes were not exclusive to the young soviet cinema; American cinema shared them, too. The Hollywood dream, Deleuze insists, was no less a dream of a transformation of the world and the creation of a new nation, a people still to come made up of all the immigrants.[3] Arising from the necessities of life, the sensorimotor schema allowed human actions, in organic representation, to extend themselves toward the hope of a new people and a new world.

This is why Deleuze can claim that, in its best moments, cinema has always been *revolutionary and Catholic.* The strangeness of such words under his pen is only superficial. The context partly explains the reference to Catholicism: Deleuze is discussing an essay by Élie Faure where Faure argued that there is a "cult" in cinema that takes over the function of the cathedrals.[4] More important than the context is the fact that Catholicism arguably plays out an aspiration toward universality, toward a becoming-world, that current processes of globalization do not exhaust. In any case, it is such a Catholic aspiration toward processes of universalization that matters for Deleuze, and if cinema is capable of replacing "the cult of the cathedrals," it is because, unlike theater, in cinema *the link between humans and the world is always at stake.* This is one consequence, and not the least significant, of an art that was from the outset an *art of the masses.* What establishes the connection between the masses and the world is *hope:* the hope for a transformation both political and ethical. Thanks to the efforts of human agency, the world will become a better place and, at the same time, new spiritual dimensions will open up within our souls. Far from opposing each other, Christian faith and revolutionary faith pick up where the other leaves off and converge toward the new to be created.

Of course, such hopes were extinguished long ago. They remain in the memory like the archival documents of a history that is no longer ours. The violence of images Eisenstein called for to awake thought has become the violence of "sex and blood," of "shocking" content in search of an infinite escalation: more and more sex and blood, more and more horror and "strong sensations," for less and less thought.[5] Such films, doubtless, have not realized Eisenstein's hopes. But this is not the only reason why the confidence of past cinema seems so naive today. There are still worse things than the mediocrity, or ignominy, of a countless number of films. Cinema's worst enemy is cinema itself. The particular power of movement-images quickly showed its double face. We know the importance fascism and Hitlerism placed on the cinematographic industry. Catholic and revolutionary faith was caught unawares by the subjection of the masses, the power of propaganda, and the staging in the service of States whose aims we know not to be exactly those of human emancipation. It was the "aestheticisation of politics," as Benjamin famously described it, that shattered the confidence in the transformative and progressive power of images.[6] The fact that brilliant artists like Leni Riefenstahl compromised themselves with the worst political regimes made it impossible to acquit cinema by an appeal to simplistic distinctions between "good" and "bad" cinema, noble art and base propaganda.[7] The shadow of the 1930s did not spare art or the arts any more than it spared culture as a whole. Cinema of time, in Deleuze's eyes, was also the response of filmmakers to the ambivalent power of movement-images, the attempt to create images that could not be hijacked, or not so quickly, from themselves in order to serve the aims of "the aestheticization of politics."[8]

But at this point we return to our initial question. Once the action-image has been broken, once revolutionary faith in a world to come has been broken, what does modern cinema give us to believe—and to live? The question has two inextricable aspects. Dialectical or teleological modes of thinking on history subordinate pure time and its various dimensions to an end to come, a *telos* to be attained. They give a direction and a sense to the events that punctuate history. The idea of revolution is a typical example of this: the new world to come regulates human actions and gives them a real significance. Even in its noblest versions, this subordination of time to history has one major shortcoming for Deleuze. It orders events and life according to a transcendental value. That the transcendence in question is secularized changes nothing. It does not matter whether it is paradise or the future of a revolution that is at issue: they function in the same way and entail the same consequences. The thought of immanence implies the rejection of any historicism and of the subordination of time to the oriented path that historicism, according to Deleuze, necessarily implies. This is the first aspect of the question. But the refusal of the category of history, and of the temporal transcendence that sustains it, cannot imply an acquiescence to the present such as it is. Confusing immanence with the affirmation of a given state of the world would not only be a misunderstanding but the worst betrayal.

The honor of thought—in art, science, or philosophy—is to resume ceaselessly the battle against prejudice and error, of course, but still more and still more decisively the battle against opinions: those opinions that we all share and that regulate our life and our convictions all the better for being barely perceivable, protected as they are by the dangerous evidence of everything that "goes without saying." Philosophy has a particular responsibility in this respect. Although it was born from Plato's will to distance himself from every *doxa,* philosophy continually reasserts the power of opinions and, still worse, places this power at the very heart of thought by falling into the trap of a veritable transcendental illusion. The force of this illusion is what leads philosophy to erect what Deleuze calls the *dogmatic image of thought,* which should be understood as a series of postulates that determine the nature of the faculty and act of thinking, de jure if not de facto.[9] Although I cannot here analyze all the aspects of this famous—and important—theme in Deleuze's ocuvre, we must nonetheless recall those aspects that concern us directly, especially because we will soon see how *Cinema 1* and *2* made this problematic evolve in respect to a decisive point.

What does the image of thought consist of, and why is it dogmatic? To put it very schematically: philosophy ascribes a nature to thought, making it a faculty that exercises itself spontaneously in pre-established harmony, so to speak, with the truth it is seeking. It may be distracted from its natural exercise and led into error by foreign forces: the body, illusions of the senses, passions, interests, and so forth. This natural attunement between thought and truth goes hand in hand with a model of knowledge that makes all cognition an act of recognition, and makes of thought itself a form of recognition. There are at least two consequences of this model of what it means to think that Deleuze deems deplorable. From the point of view of knowledge, recognition is "insignificant": of course there are constantly acts of recognition, but nothing of what is truly at stake in thought takes place in the "recognition" of an object. On the other hand, the model of recognition stops being insignificant only to become dangerous as soon as one considers the "ends which it serves." For if thinking is recognizing [*reconnaître*], what is recognized [*reconnu*] is simultaneously and inextricably an object and the values attributed to it. It is in this sense that the image of thought is dogmatic or even orthodox: it suspends every particular *doxa,* but it does so in order to retain the essential, to universalize it, and make it into a transcendental model (Deleuze, *Difference and Repetition,* 134/176). The problem with this model is that it neutralizes both sense and time. The supposedly natural agreement between thought and truth hides the essential fact that truth has no value outside "an hour and a place." Rather than ascribing to thought an autonomous exercise, a purely interior force that encounters its limit in external obstacles, Deleuze, following Nietzsche, proposes that we invert the model. It is only when thought is constrained by a necessity coming from the outside that it starts thinking; its real enemies lie within. We think not by nature but by necessity: when something in the world does us violence, and violence in this context means the shock of an encounter with what we do not know [*connaissons*] and even less recognize [*reconnaissons*]. What threatens thought is not error but the power of stupidity, of malevolence, of nonsense, powers all the more formidable since they belong to thought itself.[10]

The dogmatic image of thought would thus be philosophy's disavowal of itself or, perhaps, an example of a specifically philosophical form of stupidity. Be that as it may, it should be remarked that this disavowal, or betrayal, takes place when the power of time is forgotten. As Proust would have it—and it is therefore not surprising to find him alongside Nietzsche in Deleuze's elaboration of the theme of the image of thought—*every truth is a truth of time.*[11] But it should be noted that the first acknowledgment of the power of time is an act of resistance, an act of resistance to the *present*. Whenever philosophy reaffirms its ties with its Platonic vocation of fighting against opinions, whenever it becomes truly *critical* philosophy once again, it finds itself, according to Deleuze, alongside another form of thought—art—in the same opposition to the state of the world as it is, to a *present* that we are asked to believe is unchangeable, frozen in an immutable state of things. This is the point of encounter between philosophical writings and artistic works, their shared vocation: "They have resistance in common—resistance to death, to servitude, to the intolerable, to shame, and to the present."[12]

How then can we reconcile the absolute refusal of any temporal transcendence, of any project of transformation to be judged by the gauge of History, with the equally trenchant opposition to the present such as it is? Can one resist the present without calling for a future to come? We must, of course, specify what is meant by terms like *present* and *future* in this particular context: temporal concepts are no more univocal than other concepts.[13] The problem here, however, is not simply terminological; it is fundamental, and it is a problem that concerns all of Deleuze's philosophy, long before and well after *Cinema 1* and *2*. As early as *Nietzsche and Philosophy*, in his reading of the eternal return, Deleuze tries to articulate coherently the temporal character of all truth and the notion of critique as insubordination to the present. This is a necessary task for Deleuze, who understands the philosophy of immanence not only as an ontology but also a *critical* philosophy with an ethical bearing, as is made clear by the insistence on the notions of sense and value, as important as those of truth and falsehood.[14] This problem, which Deleuze addresses again and again throughout his oeuvre, gives rise to a complex conceptual configuration that aims at giving an account of the multiple aspects of temporality.[15] *Becoming* is one such concept: it expresses a purely immanent dimension of time, one without a determinable beginning or end and one that cannot be judged—or even experienced—according to any result attained. The ontological and ethical consistency of becoming is due to its own operation, and although it does not take place "elsewhere" than in history, although it is born in history and always falls back into it, it nonetheless does not belong to history.[16] Becoming thus begins to provide an answer, at least for Deleuze, to the question of a dimension of time that is at once immanent and irreducible to history and of a *time livable in itself,* without any messianic expectations that seem to have taken the place of revolution in philosophy as in certain kinds of politics. Yet even becoming leaves the problem of the world open and unanswered. Can we live without hope and without a grasp on the situations that surround us? What can replace the broken links of organic representation?

Modern cinema, according to Deleuze, was formed as a field of elaboration of this question, and it has explored possible answers from different directions. In undoing the sensorimotor links of the action-image in order to take the paths of images that come from time, it went beyond the crisis of the action-image toward its cause: the rupture of the link between humans and the world. But it acquires its force, as we have seen, by refusing to stop with an acknowledgment, or even a critique, of this rupture. The greatness of modern cinema lies in its capability to create other links. Italian neorealism marks the appearance of pure optical and sound situations in cinema and of characters who are no longer "actors" but seers, witnesses of a world that has become unthinkable *because* it has become intolerable—as intolerable in its immense injustices as in its daily banality. Gazes halt; they are no longer linked with "adapted responses," yet they are neither passive nor resigned. In their own way they produce the shock that Eisenstein had hoped for. Rossellini, once again exemplary for Deleuze, opens the path of modern cinema by giving art, in the face of an inhuman world, the task of *believing* and *producing belief* in the world.[17] But how then is this different from classic cinema and the Catholic and revolutionary faith that drove it? One might suspect Deleuze of substituting the "old" faith with the same "modern" faith, the only difference being that "modern" faith has renounced transforming the world. Yet in the passage from one faith to the other, a major change takes place:

The link between man and the world is broken. Henceforth, this link must become an object of belief: it is the impossible which can only be restored within a faith. Belief is no longer addressed to a different or transformed world. Man is in the world as if in a pure optical and sound situation. The reaction of which man has been dispossessed can be replaced only by belief. Only belief in the world can reconnect man to what he sees and hears. The cinema must film, not the world, but belief in this world, our only link. The nature of the cinematographic illusion has often been considered. Restoring our belief in the world—this is the power of modern cinema (when it stops being bad). Whether we are Christians or atheists, in our universal schizophrenia, *we need reasons to believe in this world.* (*C2,* 171–72/223)

What stands out in this long citation is the theme of an *immanent conversion* of faith. Faith is no longer concerned with a heavenly sphere beyond life, but neither is it concerned with the *project* of a better world to come. The object of faith is not in a temporal beyond to be attained; belief no longer fills the wait with hope, thus making it acceptable. The new faith invests the world as it is, not to justify what is intolerable, but to make us believe that although the organic form of the link that attached us to the world is broken, the link itself is not broken, and other forms of it can still be invented. Belief concerns our possibilities of life in this world, the only world we have, thus exposing yet another reason that Deleuze, despite his admiration of—and debt to—Bazin, never espoused the theme of the realist vocation of cinema. What is at stake in cinema—and in our modern condition—is not "reality." We do not doubt exterior reality or the existence of the world: our skepticism is not cognitive. We lack neither knowledge nor certainty. Of course, Bazin did not expect that realism as the privileged aesthetic form would give us more certain knowledge. He expected, rather, a more faithful gaze on beings and things, a gaze finally freed of our "spiritual dust and grime."[18] Rossellini's call for belief "in love and life" converged in his work with the phenomenological inspiration of returning to things themselves.[19] Now, Deleuze does not believe that cinema, or any other medium, has any particular ability to offer a "more adequate representation" of reality, because, quite simply, representation itself seems to him to be a bad concept. Furthermore, he does not believe that another face of the world could in itself restore our confidence. Or, to be more precise, belief is the necessary precondition of this gaze, of our gaze and of the gaze of things. What is broken with History is our *link* to the world, and the power of time in person will lead us nowhere if this link is not reestablished. Our skepticism is *ethical,* and this is why it can only be resolved *in* and *by* an act of faith. "Faith" alone can forge the link anew and give us the world once again.[20]

Deleuze is well aware of the false naivety of his position and writes that "fools laugh" in the face of our need for "an ethic or a faith."[21] Yet, for him, this belief in the world is precisely what cinema has attempted to film, from Dreyer to Antonioni, from Rossellini to Godard, from Pasolini to Rohmer, and to many other filmmakers. Thus, in its own way, cinema pursues a conversion of faith—and of philosophy—that comes from afar, but it is only because of cinema that Deleuze is first able to formulate the question of modernity in terms that are antithetical to a certain Nietzschean *doxa.* But what conversion is at issue? In the history of philosophy, it is the progressive substitution of the model of belief for that of knowledge.[22] Pascal and Kierkegaard are the two major examples: in place of the certainty of knowledge, even the minimal certainty of the Cartesian cogito, they place their bets on faith. Faith and knowledge diverge; they start following different lines; they are not opposed like "the rational and the irrational," but one can never be the foundation of the other. No knowledge of God or of the world could give us belief, and the problem with ontological proofs for the existence of God is not their poor formulation or logical untenability. Rather, their defect is originary, so to speak: they mistake their domain, because faith is not an object of knowledge but of choice. Deleuze interprets this well-known theme of Jansenism and the Reformation as a conversion of thought toward immanence. Pascal's wager or Kierkegaard's repetition are, in his eyes, a choice for the world. The faith that they follow and the choice that they assert have bearing on a form of existence, not that of God, but that of man, who, through faith, chooses to live in a different way in this world. The stakes of the wager are not salvation to come but belief in the possibilities of life.

In *Cinema 1,* Deleuze devotes several pages to the "relations of great value" that cinema and philosophy have been able to weave around this hyperbolic choice that is opposed to all morality in the name of a purer ethical demand (*C1,* 116/163). Kierkegaard's Abraham has siblings in films by Dreyer and Rossellini, of course, but also in Rohmer's *Moral Tales* or in Bresson. These films are populated by characters gripped by the necessity of a moral choice, and they live and move in a "spiritual space."[23] *Cinema 2* returns to this question and explains its bearing. The conversion from the model of knowledge to that of belief is not the exclusive concern of religion or theology. It invests all of thought. In the history of philosophy, it is pursued as much by religiously minded authors as by staunch atheists who together form "true couples": Deleuze cites Pascal and Hume, Kant and Fichte, Kierkegaard and Nietzsche, Lequier and Renouvier.[24] The reason for this is double—and symmetrical. Those who are still "pious" need faith to be assured of the possibility of life in the world; those who are atheists can no longer count on knowledge to make the world livable again. In both cases, belief is immanent; its only object and only concern are the modes of existence.

This conversion of belief is more profound and more significant than conventional rifts between religion and atheism or than debates on secularization or, conversely, on the return of the religious. Indeed, it defines our "modern condition," insofar as there is one. We "moderns" are not, according to Deleuze, in an interminable state of mourning for God and for the divine; it is not that we are unable to accept the news of the death of God, nor are we unable to wait for the "God to come," as Heidegger might maintain. In other words, modernity is not *melancholic;* it is not attended by the shadow of a lost object, nor is it split between those enlightened ones who could at least name and think their condition as impossible and unendable mourning and those blind ones plagued by maniacal triumphs.[25] We are lacking something very different: the world. We have "lost" the world, but the modality of this loss is not that of death, disappearance, distancing, or any of the notions connected with the register of mourning. The world is indeed there, but what is now lacking is the hope required to create new possibilities of life in it. The true modern problem is thus the problem of a faith that can make the world livable and thinkable once again, not in itself, but for us:

> [I]t is possible that the problem now concerns the one who believes in the world, and not even in the existence of the world but in its possibilities of movements and intensities, so as once again to give birth to new modes of existence, closer to animals and rocks. It may be that believing in this world, in this life, becomes our most difficult task, or the task of a mode of existence still to be discovered on our plane of immanence today. (*WPh*, 74–75/72)

This quotation from *What Is Philosophy?* clearly shows that the theme of belief in the world was not an occasional one, merely making a furtive appearance in the books on cinema, a one-time homage to certain "Catholic" authors.[26] All the more so because it is not a simple reprise: in *What Is Philosophy?* Deleuze significantly develops the problem of the world and of faith and, in an entirely new way, connects it with his long-standing preoccupations about the plane of immanence and the image of thought. In the last lines of *Cinema 2,* Deleuze admits that the time had perhaps come to stop asking "what is cinema?" and ask "what is philosophy?"[27] A few years later, *What Is Philosophy?*, written with Guattari, keeps this promise and begins precisely at the point where *Cinema 2* had ended. Some of the many questions that the book reopens are the direct legacy of the work on cinema. The question of the world, which was lost because it fell outside organic representation and which cannot be found again except by becoming the object of a faith, engages the question of immanence as it arises today, on our own plane, that of a modern image of thought. But for the question to take this form, there had to be a shift in Deleuze's oeuvre.

Difference and Repetition established the ontological frame of the philosophy of immanence as the *univocity* of being. The necessary condition for thinking immanence is to conceive of being as univocal rather than analogical. The opposition between the two approaches cannot be reconciled because of two decisive differences. The first one has to do with how the distribution of being is understood: analogical thought conceives of the relation between being and beings as a division of being itself, a division of that which is distributed. This is the Aristotelian model of categories, in which being is distributed in fixed genera that are held in an analogical relation to each other. In univocal thought, to the contrary, the relation of being to beings is conceived as a distribution of beings in being itself. These opposed conceptions of distribution imply two conceptions of hierarchy that are also in opposition. The analogical approach measures beings as a function of their degree of proximity or distance to a principle, whereas univocity considers beings from the point of view of their power, in Spinoza's sense of the term—their power to go beyond given limits in order to go to the end of "what they can do." Note that what is essential in univocity derives not only from the fact that being is said in a single and same sense of everything that it is said of, but from the fact that what it is said of *differs*. Univocal being is directly related to difference(s) and thus serves a necessary function in Deleuze's philosophy: making immanence and difference coincide.[28] In the history of philosophy, according to Deleuze, three thinkers laid out the understanding of being as univocal: Duns Scotus, Spinoza, and Nietzsche, who each contributed to further elaborate an ontology of immanence. The overlapping thus established between the univocity of being and immanence remains crucial for Deleuze, just as the wider ontological framework elaborated in *Difference and Repetition* continues to orient his work.[29] Nonetheless, *What Is Philosophy?* states the problem of immanence in very different terms from the outset. Immanence is now thought as necessary to and coextensive with the very exercise of philosophy rather than somehow being merely a minoritarian trend in philosophy.

In the analyses of *What Is Philosophy?* there is philosophy whenever there is immanence, and if philosophy was born in Greece, this is because, as Jean-Pierre Vernant suggests in *The Origins of Greek Thought,* the Greeks were the first to conceive of an order strictly immanent to the cosmos. Rather than writing the genealogy of the rare thinkers of immanence, Deleuze is now concerned with envisaging the whole history of philosophy from the point of view of the institution of a plane of immanence, asking for what reasons, intrinsic and external to thought, philosophy continually reproduces illusions of transcendence (*WPh*, 43–44, 49/46, 50). I would like to argue that the problem is thus stated in an entirely different manner than it is in *Difference and Repetition* and that this change in perspective is a direct consequence of *Cinema 1* and *2*. This rather abrupt hypothesis can, I hope, be confirmed convincingly if one attends to the way Deleuze defines the plane of immanence in *What Is Philosophy?* If philosophy is a creative activity, a *constructivism* as Deleuze and Guattari often call it, it needs in its exercise to produce both its own objects—concepts—and a field, a plane, a ground, a land—a chain of terms that constantly return—that will shelter them and ensure their autonomous existence. Philosophy constructs concepts and traces the plane that they will populate.[30] Consequently, the plane of immanence is neither a concept nor the sum or set of all concepts; if it were, it would lose its essential character of opening. The plane is *open*. Another essential difference from concepts is that the plane is neither thought nor thinkable but is, to the contrary, *the image of thought*, which should be understood—as it already is in *Difference and Repetition*—as the rigorous attribution of what belongs to thought de jure, not de facto. The plane of immanence as an image of thought claims *infinite movement* for this image, movement without spatiotemporal coordinates, without horizon, and more important, without determined moving bodies. Absolute movement coincides, on the one hand, with the image of thought, that is to say with thought itself, but on the other hand, it is also, inextricably, the very matter of being. It follows that the plane of immanence has two complementary aspects: Thought and Nature (*WPh*, 37–38/40–41).

If we think back to the first chapter of *Matter and Memory* and Deleuze's analysis of the Bergsonian universe of movement-matter-light-images in terms of the plane of immanence, all the traits that we have just briefly described—infinite movement as image of thought and matter of being—will sound very familiar. In *Cinema 1,* for the first time, Deleuze read Bergson—a certain Bergson—as a philosopher of immanence. In *What Is Philosophy?* the metacinematographic universe of *Matter and Memory* gives the field of immanence as such its most significant aspects. If he was absent from the line of thinkers of the univocity of being in *Difference and Repetition,* Bergson henceforward will figure alongside Spinoza:

> Spinoza is the vertigo of immanence from which so many philosophers try in vain to escape. Will we ever be mature enough for a Spinozist inspiration? It happened once with Bergson: the beginning of *Matter and Memory* marks out a plane that slices through the chaos—both the infinite movement of a substance that continually propagates itself, and the image of thought that everywhere continually spreads a pure consciousness by right. (*WPh,* 48–49/50)

Moreover, the image of thought itself has swung into immanence. *Difference and Repetition,* as we have seen, pronounced a merciless judgment on the (dogmatic) image of thought. The critique of this image was accompanied, in a perfectly symmetrical manner, by a call for philosophy to become, finally, "thought without image."[31] Of course, in *Difference and Repetition,* as in all his other works, Deleuze grants a great importance to the arts. We also find explicit references to the role that the theater and the new cinema can play in the elaboration of a new manner of making—and writing—philosophy. What changes because of *Cinema 1* and *2* is neither the value granted to arts, nor the critique of the postulates of the dogmatic image of thought such as Deleuze had analyzed them previously, but rather the conception of images and their ontological status: images have gained all sorts of speeds and movements, all sorts of depths of time. Philosophy no longer needs to understand the necessary task of struggling against its own illusions as the task of freeing itself from the image.[32] Infinite movement and image have become unified and inseparable, constituting the plane of immanence that philosophy traces as a "section of chaos." Philosophy has a vital need to trace such a plane because its own challenge is to give this plane consistency, to extract a little consistency from the chaos that undoes everything, without, for all that, giving up the infinity of movement and its speeds. It is in relation to this very struggle against chaos that *What Is Philosophy?* tries to understand the illusions that philosophy continually renews, the effects of transcendence that punctuate its whole history. It is not easy to endure infinite speeds, to give consistency to chaos, without giving up absolute movement. Transcendence is produced, according to Deleuze and Guattari, by stopping movement: it is not, or no longer, produced by the image, which is movement in itself, but by *the freeze-frame* [*arrêt sur image*].[33]

And it is also in relation to chaos that the question of the unity or plurality of the plane of immanence is envisaged. There are so many distinct images of thought in the history of philosophy because each one "sifts" chaos in a different way, each selects in a different way what belongs to thought de jure. It could not be otherwise, because no plane can embrace the whole of chaos. Consequently each plane sections chaos differently, not preventing but instead allowing concepts or even planes themselves to encounter each other, to be distributed, to regroup themselves differently in the history of philosophy, according to a logic of time that is not the logic of historicism. The time of philosophy is a stratigraphic time, just as *the* plane of immanence is interleaved (*WPh*, 50, 58/51, 58). Inseparably "image of thought" and "matter of being," composed of infinite movements and speeds, the field of immanence so closely resembles the Bergsonian universe that it is difficult to distinguish them. Deleuze called Bergson's universe a *metacinema;* one could ask if this was not his way of making cinema not only the art of the twentieth century but also a necessary part of the new image—the modern image—of thought.

▪ *Conclusion*

To conclude, let me pose the question of the status of *Cinema 1* and *2,* which should not be confused with the question about the effects produced by these two books in philosophy or in film and media studies, because it concerns first of all the relation *between* philosophy and cinema. In this respect, the very last lines of *Cinema 2* make a claim as peremptory as it is enigmatic: "Cinema's concepts are not given in cinema. And yet they are always cinema's concepts, not theories about cinema" (280/366). This assertion condenses several theses, some of which we have encountered and discussed, others that still need to be unfolded. Namely:

1. Cinema, like other arts, is a form of thought and, as such, has its autonomy. This means that the singular thought of cinema is expressed in the images it produces. On this level, cinema needs nothing else; in any case, it needs no theory that would make it an object and then apply categories derived elsewhere upon it; still less does it need a vague form of "reflection." Filmmakers, spectators, and critics of cinema reflect by themselves, and they need neither philosophy nor "theories" to do so.

2. Philosophy as exercise of thought also has its own autonomy, which means, for Deleuze, that philosophy produces specific

"objects"—concepts—and that therefore, like the arts, philosophy is a form of thought and an act of creation. But then other questions arise. What then distinguishes all these different forms of thought/creation? What types of relations can be woven between them and on what level? Indeed, the problem concerns philosophy in particular. If one calls into question, as Deleuze does, a certain ordinary division that assigns the domain of creation to the arts and the domain of reflection to philosophy, philosophy's status is what becomes enigmatic. It is easier to recognize that there is thought in works of art than to determine the field of creation that belongs to philosophy in particular, especially when this field is not closed on itself but, to the contrary, is necessarily open to what lies outside it. Hence the difficulty of the quotation above. The *philosophy* of cinema creates (if it can) its own objects—concepts—which would not exist without it, neither in the heaven of ideas nor in film images. In this sense it is not a form of reflection applied to a previously given object. Nonetheless, the philosophy *of* cinema produces, as Bergson hoped, singular concepts, in this case the singular concepts of cinema and nothing else. If there is an encounter between cinema and philosophy, it takes place on the same level, that of two forms of thought/creation. But this level is precisely what must still be clarified.

After *Cinema 1* and *2*, we know what these singular concepts are, for Deleuze, and what power the thought of images has, and we might even be able to discern something of the "soul" of cinema. On the other hand, the singularity of philosophy remains obscure. Of course, Deleuze has much to say about it. He says that it is not a theory nor a reflection exercised on previously given objects but a creative activity, and that in this activity it finds its own dignity. But the nature of the objects produced by philosophy, these strange objects called *concepts*, remains mysterious. For this reason, Deleuze ends *Cinema 2* with a question, admitting that the time has come at which one must stop asking "what is cinema?" and instead ask "what is philosophy?" A few years later, a book with this very title will begin at the exact point where *Cinema 2* ends. *What Is Philosophy?* will try to answer these suspended questions, to define the differences between forms of thought/creation that are the arts, the sciences, and philosophy, and their points of intersection. But at the center of the book is first and foremost the exercise of philosophy, the effort to think its singular essence, to determine its own objects, its history, and its geography. Deleuze always made the *encounter* an eminently philosophical theme, the transcendental condition of thought. However *Cinema 1* and *2* are judged, it must be acknowledged that a real encounter with cinema takes place in Deleuze's oeuvre, leading him in directions that, in many respects, are quite new.

Appendix

A Lost Everyday: Deleuze and Cavell on Hollywood

Deleuze loved Hollywood.[1] Filmmakers such as Ford, Hawks, Mankiewicz, Minnelli, and Wyler, to name but a few, fill the pages of *Cinema 1: The Movement-Image* and *Cinema 2: The Time-Image* no less than Bresson, Vertov, Ozu, and Rossellini. Why, then, do those who are interested in Deleuze's philosophy of the cinema hardly ever talk about Hollywood? Maybe it is because what is most striking, understandably, about these two books is the great schema they articulate around the distinction between movement-images and time-images and around the thesis of the emergence of a cinema of time, a thesis that is as powerful as it is problematic. Hollywood recedes into a prehistory where the truth of cinema as a direct presentation of time could only be, at best, anticipated. This kind of reading not only forgets that Welles, Wyler, or Mankiewicz, for Deleuze, were filmmakers of time; it also turns *Cinema 1* and *2* into a teleological narrative, oriented by a goal, which, once attained, would confine its first steps to a justified oblivion. Above all, it runs the risk of missing some of the major stakes, as well as what is essential about Deleuze's philosophy of cinema. Deleuze desired to attain "the singular essence" of cinema, that which is its own and which, belonging only to cinema, differentiates it from every other form of artistic expression.

97

He sought to produce an *ontology* of cinema by asking, thus following in the footsteps of André Bazin, "What *is* cinema?"—a question deemed by many to be outdated and beyond any hope of renewal. Nevertheless this singular essence lies in the logic of images—and nowhere else. We need to look for it in the types of images and of compositions of images that cinema produces. That is why linguistic or psychoanalytic approaches are misleading: there is nothing to be looked for on this side or the other of the filmic images, no exterior structure that would prescribe their forms. Cinema is not a language. This does not amount to saying that films are made up of "light and movements"—to use the ironic expression employed by Stanley Cavell to describe certain purely formalist conceptions of cinema in *The World Viewed*—nor to denying the narrative character of the majority of films, including the most beautiful ones, but to showing that narrativity flows from a certain way of deploying images and not the other way around.

Deleuze demonstrates this point by discussing in detail different forms of montage in early cinema, particularly in the work of Griffith, that he considers groundbreaking and exercising an ongoing influence not only on American cinema but also on Soviet and European cinema. All the technical devices introduced or developed by Griffith—the close-up, the alternate parallel montage, or the convergent montage—acquire their full significance when considered in relation to each other. Together they constitute a consistent and compelling idea of montage as what gives to films their unity. More precisely, it is a specific idea of unity that Griffith brings about: that of an organism composed of coexisting elements and whose life depends on the harmonious balance between its parts. When such a balance is shaken, when the elements of the organism enter into conflict, the unity of the organism, and hence its life, is threatened. The alternate parallel montage and the convergent montage in Griffith's films show the relations of coexistence and conflict between the elements that constitute the organic unity, the series of actions through which the unity is endangered and those through which harmony is restored. *The Birth of a Nation* recounts the story of the danger that black people would constitute to the recently acquired unity of the country, whereas in *Intolerance* it is the history of all civilizations that is depicted as an organic unity.[2]

Deleuze considers Griffith's conception of montage a "powerful organic representation" that sets the standard for American cinema, where the centrality of actions is not derived from a narrative model but rather from a logic of composition of images: "American cinema draws from it its most solid form; from the general situation to the established or transformed situation through the intermediary of a duel, of a convergence of actions. American montage is organico-active. It is wrong to criticize it as being subordinate to the narration; it is the reverse, for the narrativity flows from this conception of montage" (*CI*, 31/49).

Yet organic representation characterizes not only American cinema; Eisenstein, in his films and his theoretical writings, inscribes himself within this heritage. What he criticizes is not the organic conception of montage but the "bourgeois" and empirical idea Griffith has of an organism. In this sense Eisenstein's target is not the ideological content of Griffith's films but their form. Convergent parallel montage, for instance, presents the different elements of the organism as if they were simply coexisting next to one another—the rich *and* the poor, the blacks *and* the whites, and so on; thus when a conflict begins, when the harmony is shaken, the reason is always a personal and contingent one. The conflict, like that in *The Birth of a Nation,* can proliferate and involve whole groups, an entire nation, but it is always brought about by the actions and motives of an individual. It is this conception of the organism that Eisenstein considers a mistake: the organism's unity is not the sum of external elements merely juxtaposed to one another; rather it is produced according to laws of genesis and growth. The organism is a living unity, and the conflicts that it undergoes are not the result of personal passions but of its internal forces that break its unity in order to reproduce it at a higher level. Eisenstein thus subscribes to a conception of montage that leads from a situation to its modification through a series of actions; but the organism being a *dialectical* unity, the logic of the composition of the images must follow very different rules. The introduction of new forms of montage—the montage of opposition and of attraction—is meant to replace Griffith's approach in order to express the dialectical laws that govern the unity of the organism. Once more: Deleuze is concerned with showing that if there is a thought of cinema—if movies think (and for him, there is no doubt that this is the case)—such a power of thought expresses itself through the very images: it depends neither on the content of the narrative nor on an exterior structure that cinema, with its proper means, would then "translate." André Bazin affirmed nothing else when he wrote that "the better way of understanding *what* a film seeks to tell us is to know *how* it says it."[3]

What plays itself out in the power of organic representation, however, goes well beyond the simple affirmation that films do not subordinate themselves to narration. The question concerns, rather, the force of a model that brought about the "universal triumph" of American cinema before the war, for reasons, and this needs to be stressed, that are not simply the result of economic or commercial superiority. It is important to discern more precisely what this model consists in and where its power derives from before turning to what marks its crisis—a crisis that, for Deleuze, is irreversible, notwithstanding the success of films still produced according to these rules. The most decisive aspect of this model is its realism. Since this category is rather broad, however, we must be careful to discern the precise sense that Deleuze gives to the term *realism.* For him, cinematographic realism has two features—and only two: milieus *(environments)* and behaviors. By the term *milieus,* Deleuze aims at describing a specific way of presenting spaces and times. A "milieu" is always determined geographically, historically, and socially. Behaviors, in turn, express human affects and drives that embody themselves in consistent modes of conduct. A character bursts into tears but only when he or she finds himself or herself in a situation that is unambiguously recognized as one that inflicts pain. Thus defined, realism does not exclude the extraordinary, the fantastic, and dreams; even less does it exclude melodrama, which is, on the contrary, one of its essential forms.

One could also say that what truly defines realism, for Deleuze, is a specific notion of agency. In this cinematographic model, milieus and behaviors are the two terms of a relation that is at the same time one of dependency and of antagonism. The milieu and its forces act on the characters by constituting a context, a situation, in which they are involved and to which they have to respond. The challenge of the situation calls for actions that respond to it, thus producing a different, modified situation. The action, in the strict sense of the term, has the form of a duel, or of a series of duels—with the milieu, with others, or with oneself. This pattern is what Deleuze calls the action-form: a situation given at the beginning is transformed at the end by the means of human actions. This form unfolds in several cinematographic genres, such as the documentary, the psychosocial film, the western, or the film noir, which, no matter how different they are in other regards, all share the same conception of agency as what relates conducts to milieus.

Though I cannot go into the details of Deleuze's analysis of the films of King Vidor, Hawks, and many others, I would like to insist on one aspect that is common to all these films and that is particularly significant, in his view, for American cinema in general. Although duels get underway, as we have seen, for personal reasons, this does not mean that the question of community is absent. Quite the contrary: the hero only becomes a hero, that is to say, he or she is up to the situation and capable of responding to the challenge of the milieu, only to the extent to which he or she represents the community. It is only through the mediation of the community that an individual can become a leader and accomplish a great deed. To say it in a different way, a certain notion of the autonomy of the subject, or a certain individualism if one prefers, should not be confused with a lack of concern for the shared form of life expressed by a community.

From this perspective, though, not all communities are equivalent: in order for an individual to become a hero who represents a society in its entirety, the society must be a "healthy" one, and not all societies can meet this standard. But how is this distinction between good and bad societies made? On what grounds? Where is health to be found? For Deleuze, certainly not in any established moral norm: what constitutes the health of a community is its power to believe in its motivations, its desires, its values, its ideals and dreams: "'vital' illusions, realist illusions which are more true than pure truth" (*CI*, 148), as Deleuze writes, finding a Nietzschean inspiration in Hollywood cinema. The capacity for hope and desire is necessary to the life of a society as it is to psychic life. According to Deleuze, it would thus be pointless to reproach the American dream for its supposed naïveté: "One cannot, therefore, criticise the American dream for being only a dream: this is what it wants to be, drawing all its power from the fact that it is a dream" (*CI*, 148). Societies continually change, but they do so on the basis of a "healthy illusion" that constitutes the continuity of the nation. It is in this sense that, according to Deleuze, American cinema has shot and reshot one founding film: "Finally, the American cinema constantly shoots and reshoots a single fundamental film, which is the birth of a nation—civilisation, whose first version was provided by Griffith. It has in common with the Soviet cinema the belief in a finality of universal history; here the blossoming of the American nation, there the advent of the proletariat" (*CI*, 14/205).

The importance of the Hollywood genre of historical movies is understood by Deleuze on the backdrop of his sense that American cinema is deeply historical: it believes in history as a process with a finality, and it believes in the universality of history, its capacity to embrace in the same becoming the all of humanity. The American dream is thus no less universal than the communist dream. The American nation-civilization distinguishes itself from the old nations; it wants to be the country of all immigrants, the *new world,* but the new world is precisely the one that finally accomplishes the broken promises of the old world. In this sense America's consciousness of being a new country, of representing a new beginning in history, is not interpreted by Deleuze as a lack of historical awareness but rather as a specific sensibility to the problems posed by traditions and inheritance and one that resonates with Nietzsche's *Untimely Meditations.* Thus for Deleuze, ridicule of Hollywood's conception of history and, along with it, the American dream, is completely misplaced. The three aspects of history—monumental, antiquarian, and ethical—whose uses and abuses Nietzsche analyzed, are at the heart of these films. The monumental and antiquarian aspect—in the treatment of natural and architectural environments, in the reconstitution of clothing, trappings, and machines—shows the great moments of the history of humanity and tends to make them communicate with one another beyond temporal and geographical distances. It thus puts a universal conception of history into play in which different periods link up in a common becoming of humanity.

Once more Deleuze emphasizes that Griffith, with *Intolerance*, has created the masterpiece and paradigm of the genre of the monumental film; and, once more, he insists on the importance of Griffith for Eisenstein. Eisenstein shares the project of American social and historical cinema of staging a confrontation of epochs; he distances himself from this project only on the point of how the succession of periods, the unfolding of history, has to be understood. Different civilizations, and different phenomena of the same civilization, are not pure independent effects that one resigns oneself to merely describing—with regret, if need be—but the results of a dialectic of history that cinema must explore. This is not to say that American cinema lacks a critical dimension; quite the contrary. The monumental conception of history essentially implies an ethical moment that is necessary not only to judge the past but also, and more important, to guide the present. It is the ethical image that measures and distributes periods and civilizations, condemning injustice and looking for the powers of a new beginning, as if America should be constantly rediscovered (see *C1*, 150–51/208–9).

It is shortsighted to think that Hollywood's success results only from the power of a commercial or ideological machine, of a "factory of dreams"; its success testifies rather to the force of conviction of the organic representation it has produced. The action-form expresses a coherent and compelling conception of the relation of humans to nature and history, one that is defined by their capacity for agency. Perceptions and emotions are perfectly embodied in actions and conducts, just as there are actions and conducts to properly respond to any situation. Actions may fail and not achieve their intended goal, but they never lose their hold on the historical or natural environment. The specific realism of the action-form does not exclude, as we have seen, the fantastic and the dream, as a constitutive capacity for desire and hope that sustains both personal and collective life; further, realism, as Deleuze understands it, does not exclude a relation to *belief* (see *C2*, 171/223).

Be it "classic" or "modern," cinema, for Deleuze, has the strongest connection to belief, a connection that runs through all the history of cinema despite the changes it has otherwise undergone. More precisely, Deleuze reinterprets the questions about the nature of "cinematographic illusion," about the peculiar realism of the cinematographic medium (*C2*, 171/223) in terms of belief; not belief in "reality" though—a term that carries with it too many mistaken philosophical assumptions, namely about representation—but belief in the world.[4]

In the organic conception of montage the belief in the world, in our connection to it, takes on the form of the belief in a finality of history and in a universal becoming of humanity. It is the belief that human agency will be capable of transforming the world, both politically and morally, bringing an end to social injustice as well as reawakening a spiritual life. The vocation of cinema as an "art of the masses" sustains the hopes in its emancipatory or revolutionary power. For Deleuze, America and Soviet cinema give two different versions of such hopes that share more than what is usually assumed. It does not matter much whether the new world would be that of all immigrants or of all proletarians: it is always a new world to come, a world that brings the promise of achieving universality. The cinema of movement-images relied on such a hope; cinema's confidence in itself, in the power of images to awaken thought, was indissolubly linked to it.

These hopes, certainly, now appear dated beyond recuperation, consigned to the archives of a history long gone by. Deleuze, in his analyses of the crisis of the action-image, does not hesitate to admit this. What has determined such crisis? There is, of course, the enormous amount of bad movies produced, but that is not the most important reason. The hope that cinema could provoke, by means of the "shock" of images (as Eisenstein would claim), a new way of thinking has been dashed, first of all by the double face of its own power. The art of the masses has been used in the service of propaganda and manipulation by the state "in a sort of fascism that united Hitler with Hollywood and Hollywood with Hitler" (*C2*, 165/214), often by filmmakers who were far from mediocre. But there are other, even more decisive, reasons. It is not by chance that the crisis of the action-form occurs in the aftermath of World War II. The hope placed in the power of cinema to transform the world rested on a prior belief—the very belief so forcefully expressed by organic representation. It is this very belief that is shattered for reasons both internal and external to cinema. We no longer believe that our actions have a bearing on a global situation, that they can transform it or even simply reveal its meaning. And, accordingly, we no longer believe in the capacity of a community to have hopes and dreams powerful enough to bring about the confidence necessary to reform itself. Our ties to the world are broken, and this does not hold true only for major historical or political events, which often seem to exceed our capacity for agency, but also for our everyday life, for a form of the everyday that has faded away. *The world is lost, not in itself but for us.*

This is the end of Hollywood, a metaphysical and aesthetic end, if you like, since of course Hollywood has continued, and continues, to produce all kinds of films, but according to Deleuze, "the soul of cinema is no longer there" (*C1*, 212/278); it has left the action-image and all of its avatars behind. And with it, a specific form of the relation to time has also exhausted itself. Hollywood had imposed itself on the world thanks to the power of a cinematographic form that forcefully recapitulated—as Nietzsche had done in his own way—a conception of history: that of the nineteenth century. Yet, in Deleuze's view, there is no other: with Hollywood, the belief in universal history reaches its end. This is not to say that Deleuze is belatedly joining in on the Hegelian discourse of an "end of history." Rather, he maintains that we no longer believe in a dialectical or teleological conception of history that subordinates all dimensions of time to a single end to come, to a *telos* to be reached that would give a direction and a meaning to the events that punctuate our individual and collective lives. The idea of revolution, of a new world to come, which regulates human actions and endows them with meaning, is a major example. Put differently, time is no longer subordinate to history, to a future, near or distant, which even in its noblest versions can only function as a transcendent value. *Time replaces history.* Nonetheless, this caesura-function attributed to the aftermath of World War II hardly seems to link up with the most explicit presupposition of Deleuze's philosophy of cinema as it is declared without nuances in the foreword of *Cinema 1:* "This study is not a history of the cinema. It is a taxonomy, an attempt at the classification of images and signs" (xiv). Instead of seeing a contradiction here—as has of course been done—it seems to me that what Deleuze is doing is to study cinema from the perspective of a major event of its becoming: the emergence of a cinema of time that explores time's nonlinear, nonchronological, and nondialectical dimensions. A "history of cinema," for Deleuze, would have to be an explicitly or implicitly teleological narrative in which the developments of forms would follow the line traced by a progress or a decline, while the taxonomy Deleuze produces strictly has no hierarchy—with the exception, of course, of the fundamental difference between the "great films" and mediocre productions. Yet it would be wrong to call this difference a "hierarchy"—for Deleuze, it is the same line that separates art from nonart, in cinema as elsewhere. In this sense Deleuze is certainly a modernist. Hollywood has lost its soul, and the violence of Eisenstein's images, which were capable of making us think, has become the violence of "sex and blood," from which not much may be expected for thought. But modern cinema, as Deleuze understands it, does not resign itself to diagnosing the crisis of organic representation, to producing a satire of it, or to denouncing the invasion of image clichés. It has managed to create other forms, just as powerful, that do not renounce *belief* and *hope* but put them into play differently. Nietzsche's formula for "how we are still pious," which Deleuze uses to describe a certain spirit of cinema, concerns both classic and modern cinema. But belief has changed objects. It is in his discussion of Italian neorealism that Deleuze most explicitly develops these themes. What is the definition of *neorealism?* What do filmmakers as different as Rossellini, De Sica, Fellini, Antonioni, or Visconti have in common? Not that their films have a social content, nor even, as Bazin thought, their discovery of an enigmatic, dispersed reality yet to be deciphered. What neorealism has produced, according to Deleuze, is a new kind of images, *pure optical* and *sound* images that surge up in situations in which perception, instead of prolonging itself into action, is absorbed by the object or the situation, returns to it. Neorealism is a cinema of the seer *(voyant):*

> [T]he character has become a kind of viewer. He shifts, runs and becomes animated in vain, the situation he is in outstrips his motor capacities on all sides, and makes him see and hear what is no longer subject to the rules of a response or an action. He records rather than reacts. He is prey to a vision, pursued by it or pursuing it, rather than engaged in an action. (*C2, 3*)

The contrast with the realism of Hollywood could not be clearer. Yet this pure perception that no longer prolongs itself into action is not therefore powerless. It lets us see what we no longer recognize. Films like *Germany Year Zero* and *Europe 51* by Rossellini or *The Adventure* and *The Eclipse* by Antonioni, to name just a few, are inhabited by characters who walk around in well-known places that have nevertheless lost all familiarity. Buildings, landscapes, objects, and beings no longer let themselves be stored away in the order—or disorder—of the everyday. The apartments where people live and the streets of the cities where they are born acquire an existence of their own. They are no longer "recognized" but are perceived, as it were, for the first time. The familiar order of things, in its indifference, fades away and the objects of the world acquire a new face, reveal an existence previously unnoticed that calls for their attention and absorbs them.

In a different context, that of photography, Bazin had written: "Stripping the object of my habits and prejudices, of all of the spiritual dirt my perception has wrapped it up in, only the impassibility of the lens could render it untouched to my attention and therefore to my love."[5] It is not entirely certain if "the impassibility of the lens" still has this power—if ever it did. The proliferation of images seems, rather, to make us capable of recognizing all kinds of things, including the most "intolerable" ones, which we nonetheless tolerate rather well. But this fact takes nothing away from the demands articulated by Bazin and Deleuze; on the contrary, it shows their necessity.

But what is the link between the power of a pure perception and the problem of belief and faith? The strength of organic representation lay in expressing the ties between humans and the world, in giving to those ties a consistent form. These ties now being torn, history and the everyday seem no longer to offer any hold, and even what happens to us seems to unfold on a stage from which we are almost absent: "We do not even believe in the events which happen to us, love, or death, as if they only half concerned us" (*C2,* 173/223), as if we were only half present to ourselves, to others, and to the world we live in. What could replace our capacity to act and respond, provide it in another form such that there could be, once more, a thread tying us to what we see? According to Deleuze, there is only faith or belief. Instead of old hopes for a better world still to come, for a transfigured world, we need a belief that addresses itself to this world, the only one we have. The realism we've discussed faced injustice and the intolerable by appealing to a finality of universal history. It was only on the basis of this belief that human actions had a hold on the world and that they could offer any such hold; it was this belief that constituted the tie of humans to the world. Now, however, there is no more future to justify the present. This is where the necessity of believing comes in, the necessity of a belief more difficult than the old one—without a horizon of redemption, purely immanent, with no other object than the possibility of creating new forms of life, of reestablishing the conviction that we can inhabit the world (see *C2,* 171–73/223–24).

From Ford to Rossellini or Antonioni, the problem has changed. Instead of never having been modern—as some would claim—we have been modern, according to Deleuze, for just a short time. Or, rather, we are just beginning to understand what modernity is about. Our modernity has nothing to do with a supposed process of secularization, or disenchantment, with the death of any gods, according to a certain Nietzschean or Heideggerian doxa, or with a return of the religious. The "modern fact" is the loss of belief in the world, not a loss of belief in its existence outside of us but in our capacity to relate to it. And while cinema may well be "the modern art form par excellence," this has not always been the case: cinema was not modern from its beginning but only in its becoming. This does not imply that the connection between cinema and modernity is accidental; quite the contrary. It is not by chance that Deleuze elaborates this major thesis for the first time in his books on cinema, as if cinema, more than any other form of art or thought, had the extraordinary power to condense in its short history questions and stakes that came to it from elsewhere.

This power is not that of a brilliant abbreviation that would limit itself to summarizing external events: Deleuze is too much of a Bergsonian to believe that what comes to us as the new is merely the actualization of a possibility that has always existed. The opposite is true: it is from out of cinema that the "modern fact" is thought as the loss of belief in the world and that the modern problem becomes that of an immanent conversion of faith whose traces can then be found earlier. Already in Pascal or Kierkegaard, for instance, for whom the problem of the belief in God is so intimately linked to the problem of the mode of existence of the believer, what is truly at stake is more existence in *this* world, and its spiritual transfiguration, than salvation in the other. Nor is the question of America accidental to such an understanding of modernity. From his doubtlessly European perspective, Deleuze—more than many other "continental" philosophers—was deeply aware that "America," whatever that might be or mean, is an open question for philosophy, that the new and the old world and their relation raise problems and questions philosophy should not avoid. This is why, in my view, despite the so obviously different intellectual landscape and philosophical voices and aims, one can find an unexpected proximity between Deleuze and Stanley Cavell.

In *This New Yet Unapproachable America* Cavell asks, with Emerson, What, exactly, does "a new world" mean? From Plato to Kant, philosophy had always known two worlds; separate, distinct, yet entertaining the most intimate relations; one world, ours, was not what it ought to have been, was only the misshapen image of the other. In Emerson, Marx's hope of putting an end to the duality of worlds by transforming ours, finally measuring and forming it according to the ideal, the hope that philosophy will finally be capable of incarnating its ideals in practice, takes a surprising form. Nineteenth-century America represents, or should have represented, this caesura in human history at which the conditions for philosophy's being put into practice are given, here and now. America is the kept promise of a new world, of the only world we have; America lets all doubling disappear. Nonetheless, the promise is only half-kept. The world has become one, transcendence has disappeared, but this new and immanent world, the only world given to us, is yet unapproachable. "Until when?" is no longer a relevant question; the problem is no longer one of the future but one of the present. What separates us from the world in which we are? The new America, present and yet unapproachable, risks, according to Cavell, "to drive us mad," now that there are no more reasons keeping us away from a world that we do not yet know how to approach: "Philosophy has from Plato to Kant known of two worlds; these are plenty to know. Here and now there is no reason the other is not put into practice, brought to earth. America has deprived us of reasons. The very promise of it drives you mad, as with the death of a child."[6] Emerson's America, read by Cavell, thus asks the modern question of the tie to the world that is lacking, of a world that is lost not in itself but for us.

The great Hollywood movies of the 1930s and 1940s, of which Cavell brilliantly shows the power of thinking, certainly have a less anguished mood. Rather, these films explore what we could call promising ways of approaching the everyday, of learning how to live in the ordinary. They are experiments in Emersonian hope, if you like, both individual and collective. *That* Hollywood is lost, and with it a specific form of hope. Cinema has become modern; or, more precisely, it has entered into modernism, which certainly implies for Cavell something different from Deleuze's analyses of modern cinema as a Bergsonian-Proustian cinema of pure time. Nevertheless, what is lost with Hollywood is a form of the everyday, described in almost the same terms as those used by Deleuze, only stated from an American perspective. Let me quote from *The World Viewed:*

> We no longer grant, or take it for granted, that men doing the work of the world together are working for the world's good, or that if they are working for the world's harm they can be stopped. These beliefs flowered last in our films about the imminence and the experience of the Second World War, then began withering in its aftermath—in the knowledge, and refusal of knowledge, that while we had rescued our European allies, we could not preserve them; that our enemies have prospered; that we are obsessed with the ally who prospered and prepared to enter any pact so long as it is against him; that the stain of the atomic blood will not wash and that its fallout is nauseating us beyond medicine, aging us very rapidly. It is the knowledge, and refusal to know, that we are ceding Stalin and Hitler the permanent victories of the war (if one of them lost the old world battle, he shares the spoils of the present war of the worlds), letting them dictate what shall be meant by communism and socialism and totalitarianism, in particular that they are to be equated. (62–63)

We still have something to learn from great Hollywood movies, and in particular we still have to learn how to believe in the world, how to hope for the possibility of new forms of life, for new ties between us and the world. But to learn from these films is precisely not to repeat them; it is rather to find new ways of making experience continue.

▌ Notes

Preface to the English-language Edition

1. Bergson, *Matter and Memory*, 32.
2. Deleuze, *Difference and Repetition*, 178.

Chapter One: Images in Movement and Movement-Images

1. On the relationship between cinema, memory, and modernity, see Cavell, *The World Viewed*, esp. chapters 1 and 2, pp. 3–22; Godard, *Histoire(s) du cinéma;* as well as chapter 6 in this volume. For full references to cited works, see Works Cited.
2. See Bergson, *The Creative Mind*, 9–10, 206–7/1–2, 196–97.
3. See Deleuze, *Bergsonism*, 23, 45/13, 39; Deleuze, *Difference and Repetition*, 116–19/153–58; Deleuze, *The Logic of Sense*, 79–81/97–99.
4. Deleuze refers to forms of dance and mime before the advent of cinema, because cinema influenced other modes of artistic expression.
5. This theme will play an important role in Deleuze's analysis of cinema. See chapters 2 and 3.
6. See Bergson, *The Creative Mind*, 80/73.
7. *CE*, 310/310; Bergson, *The Creative Mind*, 167–68/158.
8. See Kuhn, *The Structure of Scientific Revolutions.*
9. The critical counterpart to this position is Bergson's hostility to Kant's effort to establish the field of the transcendental as the set of conditions of possibility of any experience. For Bergson the central distinction between the concepts of the possible and the virtual is an integral part of this problematic. For the virtual see chapter 5 in this volume.
10. See Aristotle, *Physics*, bk. 4, 218b1–219b1.
11. It is interesting that Bergson's thought continues to elicit the interest of certain scientists and epistemologists. See, e.g., Prigogine and Stengers, *La nouvelle alliance,* on the Bergsonian conception of time;

and Prochiantz, "À propos d'Henri Bergson," on Bergson's vitalism and contemporary biology.

12. This, according to Deleuze, is the sole but decisive point of intersection between Bergson and Heidegger.

13. On the status of the image see chapter 2 in this volume.

14. See Bonitzer, *Décadrages*, 79–85.

15. Deleuze refers in particular to Mitry, *The Aesthetics and Psychology of the Cinema;* and to Burch, *Theory of Film Practice.*

16. Indeed, montage alone is sufficient for this. On montage see chapter 3 in this volume.

17. The stage of "classic" theater, since modern theater, like the other arts, was affected by the evolution of cinema and often tried to collapse the frontality of the representation.

18. Bazin, *What Is Cinema?* 1:96–97/51.

Chapter Two: Cinema and Perception

1. See Heidegger, "The Age of the World Picture," in *The Question Concerning Technology and Other Essays*, 115–54. In order to draw out the connection with Deleuze, I have modified the translations of Heidegger, using "image" instead of "picture" as the translation of the German *Bild,* which can mean either.

2. One aspect of modernity so defined directly concerns the status of art. The domain of art becomes that of *aisthesis,* of *sensation,* just as the thought of art becomes a separate discipline that is in fact called aesthetics. See also Heidegger, *Nietzsche.* On this point, as on many others, Deleuze takes a very different path from Heidegger by increasingly orienting himself toward a conception of art as creation of sensations. This gesture is more complex than a simple opposition to Heidegger, since for Deleuze sensations are not the correlate of any subject but are veritable *beings in themselves,* endowed with an autonomous existence. See Deleuze, *Francis Bacon; C1,* chapters 6 and 7; and *WPh,* 91–93/87–89. One finds surprisingly similar analyses in the few pages that Levinas devotes to art, in which art is what liberates sensations and gives them their own existence. See Levinas, *Existence and Existents,* 46–47/85–86.

3. Heidegger, "The Age of the World Picture," in *The Question Concerning Technology and Other Essays,* 129.

4. One of the rare texts in which Heidegger evokes cinema is "A Dialogue on Language, between a Japanese and an Inquirer," in *On the*

Way to Language, 16–17, where there is a short exchange on Kurosawa's *Rashomon* (1950).

5. The world given to be seen by a spectator-subject is also one of the points of departure for Stanley Cavell in his reflections on cinema. But because for Cavell, as for Deleuze, representation is a completely inadequate category for thinking cinema (even the photographic support of film is not a "representation" but rather a "transcription" of reality), the questions that Cavell asks of cinema as a "world viewed" move in a very different direction than does Heidegger's conception of modernity. What is at issue is not the subject of representation but a moral skepticism that concerns the relation between humans and the world. See Cavell, *The World Viewed;* and chapter 6 in this volume.

6. For a recent, detailed introduction to *Matter and Memory,* see Worms, *Introduction à "Matière et mémoire" de Bergson.*

7. The re-elaboration of the status of transcendental subjectivity is a theme that runs through Husserl's whole oeuvre. For a paradigmatic text on this see Husserl's *Cartesian Meditations.*

8. See *C1,* 56/83–84.

9. See *C1,* 59/87. Cinema led Deleuze to read Bergson in a different way. However important Bergson is for Deleuze's thought, before the books on cinema Deleuze did not place him in the lineage of philosophers of immanence. See chapter 6 in this volume.

10. Deleuze sees in *Duration and Simultaneity* not a misplaced effort to correct Einstein's theory of relativity but rather Bergson's attempt to start a dialogue with the new science with the aim of producing a new philosophy. In other terms, *Duration and Simultaneity* is the result of an encounter between philosophy and science that nonetheless respects the autonomy of the two different forms of thought. See *C1,* 60/88–89.

11. See Sartre, *L'imagination,* 42–70; and *C1,* 61n18/90n17.

12. See *C1,* 61–62/91; and *MM,* 35–36/32–33.

13. Our relation to space and time is a function of this: "Perception is master of space in the exact measure in which action is master of time" (*MM,* 32/29).

14. For a study of Merleau-Ponty's complex relationship to Bergson see Barbaras, *Le tournant de l'expérience,* esp. 33–61.

15. Bergson's explicit target is Kant's project of establishing the limits for the legitimate use of the faculties. For Bergson, Kant's first error is to mistake for the very nature of our spirit something that is merely a result of "habits" of the intelligence, dictated by the needs of life (see *MM,* 184/205).

16. *MM,* 184/205.

17. Deleuze, *Bergsonism,* 28/19.

18. For an interpretation of Vertov's role in Deleuze's book, see also Zourabichvili, "The Eye of Montage."

19. "Kino-eye uses every possible means in montage, comparing and linking all points in the universe in any temporal order, breaking, when necessary, all the laws and conventions of film construction" (Vertov, *Kino-Eye,* 88).

20. See Mitry, *Histoire du cinéma muet,* 3:256. Cited in *C1,* 81/117.

21. See Klee, "Credo du créateur," in *Théorie de l'art moderne,* 34. For Deleuze's commentaries, see *A Thousand Plateaus,* 342–43/422–23; and *Francis Bacon,* 71–72/57–58, where the problem shared by all arts is in fact designated as that of giving visible or sensible form to forces that, in themselves, are neither.

22. Neither Bergson nor Deleuze use the expression "pragmatic perception"; nonetheless, it seems to me an adequate description of what is at issue for the two philosophers.

23. See Aristotle, *Physics,* bk. 4, 218b–219b. On the different conceptions of time engaged by montage, see *C1,* 29–31/46–47; and *C2,* 34–50.

24. See Rancière, *La fable cinématographique,* 14–21.

25. For the most systematic exposition of Deleuze's questioning of the category of representation, see Deleuze, *Difference and Repetition,* 28–69/43–94.

26. See *C2,* 171–73/222–25; and chapter 6 in this volume.

27. This is Deleuze's Platonism: his deep conviction that philosophy lives off the battle against powers of opinion. On this point see Marrati, "Contro la doxa."

28. Chapters 6 and 7 of *C1,* which unfortunately cannot be analyzed in detail here.

29. See Epstein, *Écrits,* 146–47, cited by Deleuze in *C1,* 96/136.

30. On the question of expression, see Deleuze, *Expressionism in Philosophy: Spinoza;* Deleuze, *Foucault,* 31–34/38–41; and Deleuze, *A Thousand Plateaus,* 85–91/109–16.

31. For this project, Deleuze will take Peirce's semiology as a guide, as it provides a classification of signs that cannot be reduced to the model of Saussurean linguistics.

32. Indeed, for Deleuze, the postwar period functions as a temporal—and historical, in the strong sense of the word—scansion between

"classic" cinema, structured around movement-images, and the "modern" cinema of time-images.

Chapter Three: The Montage of the Whole

1. "The great directors of the cinema may be compared, in our view, not merely with painters, architects and musicians, but also with thinkers. They think with movement-images and time-images instead of concepts" (*C1*, ix/7–8).

2. See *C2*, 25–30/38–42. It is impossible, here, to recapitulate all the debates on structural linguistics and its application to cinema. For a good historical perspective on these questions, see Jay, *Downcast Eyes*, 435–91; and Casetti, *Theories of Cinema*, esp. 89–93, 132–78.

3. See *C2*, 27n5/41n5, where Deleuze gives as an example of this underestimation of images the fact that Christian Metz, in order to distinguish photography from cinema, calls on narrativity rather than movement. See Metz, *Film Language*, 45/53.

4. See *C1*, 32–35/50–57; and Eisenstein, *Film Form*.

5. See Merleau-Ponty, *Sens et non-sens*, 72; and *C1*, 155/214, where Deleuze analyzes the techniques of the Actors Studio during Kazan's time.

6. On F. Scott Fitzgerald, see also Deleuze and Guattari, *A Thousand Plateaus*, 194ff/254ff.

7. Most of Frank Capra's films exemplify the need for a community to struggle in order to constantly renew and reenact its values and dreams.

8. See *C2*, 171/222; as well as Deleuze, *Essays Critical and Clinical*, 3–5/14–16; Deleuze and Parnet, *Dialogues*, 36–38/47–49; and Deleuze and Guattari, *WPh*, 98–99/94–95.

9. See *C1*, 149n10/206n9; and Nietzsche, *Untimely Meditations*, 57–123.

10. *C2*, 171–74/222–25; and chapter 6 in this volume.

Chapter Four: Postwar Cinema

1. Bazin, *Bazin at Work*, 124; Bazin, *Qu'est-ce que le cinéma?* 1:204–5.

2. See Bazin, "The Evolution of the Language of Cinema," in *What Is Cinema?* 1:23–40/63–81.

3. Bazin, *Bazin at Work,* 124; *Qu'est-ce que le cinéma?* 1:206 (translation modified).

4. See Bazin, *What Is Cinema?* 1:36/75–76.

5. Bazin, *What Is Cinema?* 1:15/14.

6. On recognition as a false model of thought, see Deleuze, *Difference and Repetition,* 134–36/176–78; and chapter 6 in this volume.

7. *What Is Cinema?* 1:15/16. Bazin's remarks concern photography, but they are also valid for his approach to the realist vocation of cinema, as for what Deleuze writes about the gaze in Italian neorealism.

8. In chapter 5 we will see how Bergson's theory of memory intervenes decisively on this point.

9. Or of what, in Japan, defines Ozu's cinema.

10. Deleuze never wavered on this point: from *Nietzsche and Philosophy* to *Essays Critical and Clinical,* there is an absolute continuity, and both philosophy and art are born and can save their honor only in continually renewing the struggle against the power of established opinions.

11. See *C1,* 119–20/168–69. On the importance of the concept of any-space-whatever in Deleuze's philosophy of cinema, see Bensmaïa, "L'espace quelconque comme personage conceptual."

12. Notably American literature and the French *nouveau roman.*

13. Pasolini introduced this term to describe Antonioni's framing. See Pier Paolo Pasolini, "'The Cinema of Poetry,'" in *Heretical Empiricism,* 179–180.

14. *C2,* 36–37/53–54, 173–75/223–25.

15. For a recent example see Rancière, "D'une image à l'autre? Deleuze et les âges du cinéma," in *La fable cinématographique,* 145–63.

16. Just as foreign, it goes without saying, as all prophesies of the happy future of capitalism triumphant.

17. On the concept of the event see also Deleuze, *The Logic of Sense,* esp. series 21, 23, and 24; and Deleuze, *The Fold,* esp. chapter 6.

Chapter Five: The Time-Image

1. Quoted by Deleuze in *C2,* 35/51.

2. See Epstein, *Écrits,* 184–89, cited in *C2,* 36/53. In the same context, Deleuze also refers to Jean-Louis Schefer's book, *L'homme ordinaire du cinéma,* where the author stresses cinema's particular aberrant movements and their capacity to give a direct perception of time.

3. *C2*, 38/55. On this point, as on many others, Deleuze places himself within the legacy of Bazin, who had credited Welles with creating a true "condensing time" in *Citizen Kane*. See *What Is Cinema?* 1:36/76. But the valorization of a cinema of time does not take the form of an alternative between shot and montage for Deleuze. According to Bazin, the shot, and in particular the sequence shot, can restore the power of time to images themselves, whereas montage has a tendency to cut up the series of images logically and thus to give an analytical presentation of events in which time is reduced to a purely logical function. See "The Virtues and Limitations of Montage" and "The Evolution of the Language of Cinema," both in *What Is Cinema?* 1:41–52/48–61, 1:23–40/63–80. For all the reasons we have already seen, Deleuze cannot subscribe to this argument, which resembles Bergson's critique of cinema. The alternative between shot and montage is a superficial one, and, from the point of view of cinematographic theory, Deleuze is much closer to Tarkovsky, who sees temporal rhythm as the very nature of cinema and who, even as he refuses, like Bazin, to make montage the fundamental operation, believes that the weight of time fixed in shots is then assembled by montage. Rather than opposing montage to the shot, it is thus a matter of creating a montage that is itself made of temporal rhythms. See Tarkovsky, "The Film Image," in *Sculpting in Time*, 104–63; and *C2*, 42–43/60–61.

4. Because images are able to show time directly, modern montage no longer links them in a chronological order of before and after. Again following Tarkovsky, Deleuze sees in "modern" montage an effort to articulate relations to time and different temporal rhythms. Likewise, the conception of the interval between images changes. When one image need no longer follow another organically, the interval is no longer a negative moment that must merely be surmounted but takes on a value in itself, as in Godard's cinema. See *C2*, 213–14/277–79.

5. In *Gilles Deleuze's Time Machine*, one of the best books devoted to Deleuze's philosophy of cinema, D. N. Rodowick grants Bergson a central role in *Cinema 1*, while claiming that *Cinema 2* is more influenced by Nietzsche and that the time-image is developed on the basis of a "crisis of truth" and of the sudden appearance of the "powers of the false" (see esp. 121–38). See also, by the same author, "La critique ou la vérité en crise." In effect, these themes are very important, but it still seems to me that Bergson's theses on time play the same structuring role in *Cinema 2* as those on movement play in *Cinema 1* and that their articulation is decisive for Deleuze's whole project.

6. See Bergson, *MM*, 103–5/113–16; and Bergson, *Mind-Energy,* 136–38.

7. *C2,* 44/62; see also Deleuze, *Difference and Repetition,* 70–77/96–104.

8. See Alain Robbe-Grillet, "Time and Description in Fiction Today," in *For a New Novel,* 143–56/123–34.

9. The concept of the virtual plays a central role in Deleuze's philosophy, as in Bergson's, and appears in diverse contexts. Let us note from the outset that it must not be confused with the notion of the possible: the virtual, as is already the case in Bergson, is opposed to the actual but, unlike the possible, is perfectly real. The possible is thought of as identical to the real, except that it lacks existence. The virtual, to the contrary, has its own reality, but it is only actualized when it produces a line of differentiation. This is why Bergson made the virtual the reality of time as duration, as the constant creation of the new. See, among the numerous texts on this subject, "Bergson, 1859–1951" in Deleuze, *Desert Islands and Other Texts,* 22–31/37–42 (originally published in *Les philosophes célèbres,* ed. Maurice Merleau-Ponty [Paris: Éditions d'Art Lucien Mazenod, 1956]); Deleuze, *Bergsonism,* 54–56/50–53; *C2,* 41/59; Deleuze, *Difference and Repetition,* 203–7/272–76; Deleuze and Parnet, *Dialogues,* 179–85; and, more specifically in relation to cinema, Deleuze, *Negotiations, 1972–1990,* 65–67/93–95. On the concept of the virtual in Bergson, see Pearson, *Philosophy and the Adventure of the Virtual.*

10. See Husserl, *On the Phenomenology of the Consciousness of Internal Time,* pt. 1, sec. 2, 21–75/31–93.

11. "The past does not follow the present that is no longer, it coexists with the present it was. The present is the actual image, and *its* contemporaneous past is the virtual image, the image in a mirror" (*C2,* 79/106). See also Deleuze, *Bergsonism,* 58–61/54–57; and the 1956 article "Bergson, 1859–1941," in Deleuze, *Desert Islands and Other Texts,* 22–31/28–42.

12. See Bergson, *Time and Free Will: An Essay on the Immediate Data of Consciousness,* chapter 2, 75–139/56–104.

Chapter Six: Images and Immanence

1. Among Deleuze's numerous texts on this subject, see *Proust and Signs,* 46–48/58–60; *The Logic of Sense,* series 21–25 (148–80/175–211); and *Difference and Repetition,* 70–96/96–128.

2. Deleuze explicitly asserts that there is no aesthetic hierarchy what-

soever between classic and modern cinema (see *C2*, 270/354). But what is more interesting is that there could be no hierarchy: on the one hand, the choice was made from the outset (what Deleuze calls "cinema" comprises the great films); on the other hand, and above all, the end of art is never in itself, and in this sense aesthetic evaluations have no importance whatsoever. In other words, the only division that counts is the one between art and nonart, between works that are true acts of creation and the rest. Within the domain of works, aesthetic judgment is no longer relevant because the aim of art is not art but *life* (see, e.g., Deleuze and Parnet, *Dialogues*, 47–51/59–63; and "Literature and Life," in *Essays Critical and Clinical*, 1–6/11–17). Deleuze's insistent and sometimes obsessive affirmation of the value of creation is in perfect accordance with his "philosophy of life." Creating is always creating the new, which in turn is nothing other than a (new) possibility of life.

3. Chaplin's speech at the end of *The Great Dictator* (1940), a call for the freedom and solidarity of all peoples, is a famous example of this, but it is far from an isolated case. Hollywood is inscribed in the Anglo-American tradition of empiricism and pragmatism as an open field of experimentation (which does not stop it from lapsing, on occasion, into the worst effects of propaganda). See Deleuze, *Essays Critical and Clinical*, 4ff/14ff; Deleuze and Parnet, *Dialogues*, 36/47; and Deleuze and Guattari, *What Is Philosophy?* 103–6/99–101. On the relationship between pragmatism and a conception of America as "always to come," see Rorty, *Social Hope;* and Cavell, *This New Yet Unapproachable America,* esp. the chapter "Finding as Founding," devoted to Emerson (77–118).

4. See *C2*, 171/222; and Faure, "Introduction à la mystique du cinéma," in *Fonction du cinéma*, 50. On the world-becoming, see Guénoun, *Hypothèses sur l'Europe*, 293–97; and Derrida, "Faith and Knowledge."

5. The almost ritualistic repetition of debates on violence in television, in film, in video games, etc. seems, unfortunately, to confirm this.

6. See Benjamin, "The Work of Art in the Age of Its Technical Reproducibility: Third Version," in *Selected Writings*, 4:269.

7. See *C2*, 164–65/213–14, 263–65/343–46. See also Daney, *La rampe;* and Kracauer, *From Caligari to Hitler.*

8. This problem, shared by all postwar cinema, becomes almost the sole theme in the work of filmmakers like Syberberg and Straub. See *C2*, 264–71/344–54.

9. The theme of the dogmatic image of thought appears first in

Deleuze, *Nietzsche and Philosophy,* 103–10/118–26; it is taken up in Deleuze, *Proust and Signs,* 107–15/115–24; and becomes the object of a long and important chapter in Deleuze, *Difference and Repetition* (chapter 3: "The Image of Thought," 129–67/169–217).

10. See, in particular, Deleuze, *Difference and Repetition,* 149–53/194–98.

11. See Deleuze, *Proust and Signs,* 94/115.

12. *WPh,* 110/105 (translation modified). Deleuze had already written about the "mysterious" link between creation and resistance in the lecture he gave for the students of La Femis, France's national film school, on March 17, 1987: *Qu'est-ce que l'acte de creation* (available on VHS, Éd. Femis).

13. Deleuze and Guattari establish a strict relation between Nietzsche's *untimeliness* and Foucault's *actual;* see *WPh,* 111–13/106–8.

14. On the question of ethics in Deleuze's philosophy, see Smith, "The Place of Ethics in Deleuze's Philosophy."

15. In this configuration, the *event* is a determinant concept. For a good analysis of the role of this concept in different aspects of Deleuze's thought, see Zourabichvili, *Deleuze: Une philosophie de l'événement,* esp. 19.

16. See *WPh,* 110/106; and Deleuze, *Negotiations, 1972–1990,* 170–71/230–31.

17. See *C2,* 171/222; *WPh,* 170/161; and Rossellini, in *La politique des auteurs,* 65.

18. Bazin, *What Is Cinema?* 1:15/16.

19. On Bazin's oeuvre see Casetti, *Theories of Cinema.*

20. "For it is not in the name of a better or truer world that thought captures the intolerable in this world, but, on the contrary, it is because this world is intolerable that it can no longer think a world or think itself. The intolerable is no longer a serious injustice, but the permanent state of a daily banality. . . . Which, then, is the subtle way out? To believe, not in a different world, but in a link between man and the world, in love or life, to believe in this as in the impossible, the unthinkable" (*C2,* 169–70/221).

21. *C2,* 173/225. If Deleuze has often been misunderstood, he also has "allies" in places he would never have thought to look. Stanley Cavell's philosophy of cinema is oriented by the attempt to think the essential relation of cinema to reality and to the world, thus carrying on the legacy of Bazin and Panofsky, yet without founding it on a theory of

representation. Cinema represents nothing; rather, it allows us to see a world from which we are absent. In this sense, cinema is an image of skepticism, but of a skepticism whose stakes are moral rather than cognitive because it refers us to the possibility (or the lack of possibility) of a participatory relation to the world. See Cavell, *The World Viewed.* For a French perspective on Cavell's philosophy of cinema, see Laugier and Cerisuelo, *Stanley Cavell.*

22. Although the genealogy he establishes differs in part from Deleuze's, Richard Rorty analyzes the same displacement, in order to maintain it, in *Philosophy and Social Hope.* Looking beyond Rorty's book in particular, a question emerges regarding the convergence between the multifarious tradition of American pragmatism and certain aspects of Deleuze's philosophy, a convergence that would need to be studied. For one of the rare texts that think in this direction, see Patton, "Redescriptive Philosophy."

23. Bresson's fragmented spaces are a good example, according to Deleuze, of cinema that films time as open and as a dimension of spirit. See *C1,* 116–17/164–65.

24. See *C2,* 171n30/224n30.

25. See Freud, "Mourning and Melancholia," in *The Standard Edition of the Complete Psychological Works of Sigmund Freud,* 14:239–58.

26. It should be emphasized in this context that Deleuze does not renounce the other essential element of the catholic and revolutionary vocation of cinema: *the people.* The concept of the people, like that of the world, is rearticulated in the new configuration of cinema and plays just as important a role as in classic cinema. If I give it less space in this book, this is because *Cinema 1* and *2* essentially repeat the analyses already sketched in *Kafka* and in *A Thousand Plateaus,* which, moreover, can be found in a nearly identical form up to and including *Essays Critical and Clinical.* The classic model of the coming to consciousness of a people, which presupposes the unity of the people, is marked by an irreversible failure. Modern cinema, even and especially when it aims to be very political and engaged, is constituted, according to Deleuze, on the basis of this failure, and instead of the becoming conscious of a people that is *one* and destined to be victorious, Deleuze substitutes a multiplicity of peoples, fragmentary and minoritarian (see *C2,* 220–24/286–91, on Rocha's films). Recognizing the fact that there is not a unity, neither de jure nor de facto, of the people as subject of power does not entail any renunciation of politics; on the contrary, it implies a change of "problem," a

different manner of thinking and acting politically. "The people is lacking," as Klee and Kafka had already remarked (see Klee, "Conférence d'Iéna," of Jan. 26, 1924, in *On Modern Art, 55/33*; and Kafka, *The Diaries of Franz Kafka*). Deleuze repeatedly adopts this as his own, insisting on the fact that the people that is lacking—and that philosophy, like the arts and literature, can only hope for—is an eternally *minor* people: "a bastard people, inferior, dominated, always in becoming, always incomplete" (*Essays Critical and Clinical, 4/14*). If the problem must be changed, this is not because the project of constituting the people as subject of people is revealed to be impossible to realize but because the one and sovereign people, like the cinema of movement-images, has shown its double face. In Deleuze's eyes, we can no longer separate the revolutionary dream—whether American or communist—from its monstrous accomplishments, without recognizing the fact that every politics that aims to constitute the identity of a subject of power, even when it takes an "oppressed subject" as the point of departure, can only reproduce the effects of oppression of all identity politics (see *C2*, 215–17/281–83; on the concepts of majority, minority, and becoming-minority, see Deleuze and Guattari, *A Thousand Plateaus*, in particular plateaus 4 and 10). The people is thus necessarily minor, and as minor it cannot stop becoming, resisting the present, investing this world with hope, and creating new forms of existence in it. This question engages all of Deleuze's reflections on politics and exceeds the scope of this book. For an analysis of the political significance of Deleuze's thought, see Patton, *Deleuze and the Political;* Etienne Balibar, "Les trois concepts du politique," in *La crainte des masses,* in particular 39–53; Zourabichvili, "Deleuze et le possible (de l'involontarisme en politique)"; Marrati, "Against the Doxa."

27. *C2*, 280/366. On the reasons for the slippage from one question to the other, see the conclusion of this volume.

28. See Deleuze, *Difference and Repetition*, 35–42/53–61. For a more detailed analysis of the status of the univocity of being in Deleuze, see Marrati, "L'animal qui sait fuir."

29. See, e.g., Deleuze and Guattari, *A Thousand Plateaus*, 254/311.

30. *WPh*, 7, 36/12, 39. Concepts are distributed on the plane without dividing it, precisely according to the principle of the univocal distribution of being.

31. Deleuze, *Difference and Repetition*, 132, 167, 276/173, 217, 354.

32. If Deleuze hesitates between the call for a "thought without image" (which can also be found in *A Thousand Plateaus*, 376/467) and

the hope of creating a "new image of thought" (which first appears in *Nietzsche and Philosophy* and *Proust and Signs*), what is decisive in *What Is Philosophy?* is that images of thoughts are multiplied and are henceforth endowed with the same mobility and depth of time as those of cinema.

33. It is significant that in this context Deleuze makes an explicit reference to Bellour's work on cinema; see *WPh*, 47.

Appendix

1. This appendix is based on a lecture presented at the University of Chicago in the spring of 2006. It further develops certain analyses of the present volume about Deleuze's interest in Hollywood cinema and offers some new perspectives on that issue.

2. For a more detailed analysis of this point, and specifically for the reasons why Griffith's conception of montage depends on the action-form, see chapter 3 of the present volume.

3. Bazin, *What Is Cinema?* 1:30 (translation modified). Bazin was discussing Italian neorealism.

4. For a more detailed analysis of Deleuze's critique of representation, see chapter 2 of the present volume.

5. See Bazin, *What Is Cinema?* 1:15 (translation modified).

6. Cavell, *This New Yet Unapproachable America,* 95.

.

▌ Works Cited

Works by Gilles Deleuze

Bergsonism. Trans. Hugh Tomlinson and Barbara Habberjam. New York: Zone, 1988. Translation of *Le bergsonisme.* Paris: PUF, 1966.

Cinema 1: The Movement-Image. Trans. Hugh Tomlinson and Barbara Habberjam. Minneapolis: University of Minnesota Press, 1986. Translation of *Cinéma 1: L'image-mouvement.* Paris: Minuit, 1983.

Cinema 2: The Time-Image. Trans. Hugh Tomlinson and Robert Galeta. Minneapolis: University of Minnesota Press, 1989. Translation of *Cinéma 2: L'image-temps.* Paris: Minuit, 1985.

Desert Islands and Other Texts, 1953–1974. Ed. David Lapoujade. Trans. Michael Taormina. Los Angeles: Semiotext(e), 2004. Translation of *L'île déserte et autres texts: Textes et entretiens, 1953–1974.* Paris: Minuit, 2002.

Difference and Repetition. Trans. Paul Patton. New York: Columbia University Press, 1994. Translation of *Différence et répétition.* Paris: PUF, 1969.

Essays Critical and Clinical. Trans. Daniel W. Smith and Michael A. Greco. Minneapolis: University of Minnesota Press, 1997. Translation of *Critique et clinique.* Paris: Minuit, 1993.

Expressionism in Philosophy: Spinoza. Trans. Martin Joughin. New York: Zone, 1992. Translation of *Spinoza et le problème de l'expression.* Paris: Minuit, 1968.

The Fold: Leibniz and the Baroque. Trans. Tom Conley. Minneapolis: University of Minnesota Press, 1993. Translation of *Le pli: Leibniz et le baroque.* Paris: Minuit, 1988.

Foucault. Trans. and ed. Seán Hand. Minneapolis: University of Minnesota Press, 1988. Translation of *Foucault.* Paris: Minuit, 1986.

Francis Bacon: The Logic of Sensation. Trans. Daniel W. Smith. Minneapolis: University of Minnesota Press, 2003. Translation of *Francis Bacon: Logique de la sensation.* 1981. Paris: Le Seuil, 2002.

Works Cited

The Logic of Sense. Trans. Mark Lester and Charles Stivale. New York: Columbia University Press, 1990. Translation of *Logique du sens.* Paris: Minuit, 1969.

Negotiations, 1972–1990. Trans. Martin Joughin. New York: Columbia University Press, 1995. Translation of *Pourparlers.* Paris: Minuit, 1990.

Nietzsche and Philosophy. Trans. Hugh Tomlinson. New York: Columbia University Press, 1983. Translation of *Nietzsche et la philosophie.* Paris: PUF, 1962.

Proust and Signs. Trans. Richard Howard. Minneapolis: University of Minnesota Press, 2000. Translation of *Proust et les signes.* 1964. Expanded ed. Paris: PUF, 1970.

Works by Gilles Deleuze and Félix Guattari

Kafka: Toward a Minor Literature. Trans. Dana Polan. Minneapolis: University of Minnesota Press, 1986. Translation of *Kafka. Pour une littérature mineure.* Paris: Minuit, 1975.

A Thousand Plateaus: Capitalism and Schizophrenia. Trans. Brian Massumi. Minneapolis: University of Minnesota Press, 1987. Translation of *Mille plateaux.* Paris: Minuit, 1980.

What Is Philosophy? Trans. Hugh Tomlinson and Graham Burchell. New York: Columbia University Press, 1994. Translation of *Qu'est-ce que la philosophie?* Paris: Minuit, 1991.

Works by Gilles Deleuze and Claire Parnet

Dialogues. Trans. Hugh Tomlinson and Barbara Habberjam. New York: Columbia University Press, 1987. Partial translation of *Dialogues avec Claire Parnet* (1977).

Dialogues II. Trans. Hugh Tomlinson and Barbara Habberjam. New York: Columbia University Press, 2002. Partial translation of *Dialogues avec Claire Parnet* (1996).

Dialogues avec Claire Parnet. 1977. Expanded ed. Paris: Flammarion, 1996.

Works by Henri Bergson

Creative Evolution. Trans. Arthur Mitchell. New York: Henry Holt, 1931. Translation of *L'évolution créatrice.* 1907. 8th ed. Paris: PUF, 1999.

The Creative Mind. Trans. Mabelle L. Andison. New York: Greenwood, 1968. Translation of *La pensée et le mouvant.* 1934. 14th ed. Paris: PUF, 1999.

Matter and Memory. Trans. Nancy Margaret Paul and W. Scott Palmer. New York: Zone Books, 1988. Translation of *Matière et mémoire.* 1896. 5th ed. Paris: PUF, 1997.

Mind-Energy. Trans. H. Wildon Carr. New York: Henry Holt, 1920. Translation of *L'énergie spirituelle.* 1919. 6th ed. Paris: PUF, 1999.

Time and Free Will: An Essay on the Immediate Data of Consciousness. Trans. F. L. Pogson. New York: Macmillan, 1928. Translation of *Essai sur les données immédiates de la conscience.* 1889. 6th ed. Paris: PUF, 1998.

Other Works

Aristotle. "Physica (Physics)." In *The Basic Works of Aristotle,* ed. Richard McKeon, 218–397. New York: Modern Library.

Balibar, Étienne. *La crainte des masses.* Paris: Galilée, 1997.

Barbaras, Renaud. *Le tournant de l'expérience.* Paris: Vrin, 1998.

Bazin, André. *Bazin at Work: Major Essays and Reviews from the Forties and Fifties.* Ed. Bert Cardullo. Trans. Alain Piette and Bert Cardullo. New York: Routledge, 1997.

———. *What Is Cinema?* Ed. and Trans. Hugh Gray. 2 Vols. Berkeley: University of California Press, 1967, 1971. Translation of *Qu'est-ce que le cinéma?* Paris: Les Éditions du Cerf, 1958.

Benjamin, Walter. *Selected Writings.* 4 vols. Ed. Howard Eiland and Michael W. Jennings. Cambridge, MA: Harvard University Press, 2003.

Bensmaïa, Réda. "L'espace quelconque comme personnage conceptual." *Iris* 23 (spring 1997): 25–36.

Bonitzer, Pascal. *Décadrages.* Paris: Cahiers du cinéma, 1995.

Burch, Noël. *Theory of Film Practice.* Trans. Helen R. Lane. Princeton, NJ: Princeton University Press, 1981. Translation of *Praxis du cinéma.* Paris: Gallimard, 1959.

Casetti, Francesco. *Theories of Cinema, 1945–1995.* Austin: University of Texas Press, 1999.

Cavell, Stanley. *This New Yet Unapproachable America.* Albuquerque: Living Batch, 1989.

———. *The World Viewed: Reflections on the Ontology of Film.* New York: Viking, 1971.

Daney, Serge. *La rampe.* Paris: Gallimard/Cahiers du Cinéma, 1983.

Derrida, Jacques. "Faith and Knowledge: The Two Sources of 'Religion' at the Limits of Reason Alone." In *Acts of Religion,* 40–100. Routledge: London, 2002.

Eisenstein, Sergei. *Film Form.* New York: Harcourt, Brace, 1949.

Epstein, Jean. *Écrits.* Vol. 1. Paris: Seghers, 1974.

Faure, Élie. *Fonction du cinéma.* Geneva: Gonthier, 1963.

Freud, Sigmund. *The Standard Edition of the Complete Psychological Works of Sigmund Freud.* 14 vols. London: Hogarth Press, 1953–1974.

Godard, Jean-Luc. *Histoire(s) du cinéma.* 4 vols. Paris: Gallimard, 1998.

Guénoun, Denis. *Hypothèses sur l'Europe.* Paris: Circé, 2000.

Heidegger, Martin. *Nietzsche.* 4 vols. Ed. David Farrell Krell. San Francisco: HarperCollins, 1991.

———. *On the Way to Language.* 1959. Trans. Peter D. Hertz. New York: Harper and Row, 1971.

———. *"The Question Concerning Technology" and Other Essays.* Trans. William Lovitt. New York: Harper and Row, 1977.

Husserl, Edmund. *Cartesian Meditations.* Trans. Doiron Cairns. Dordrecht: Kluwer, 1964.

———. *Leçons pour une phénoménologie de la conscience intime du temps.* 1928. Paris: PUF, 1964.

———. *Méditations cartésiennes.* 1931. Paris: Vrin, 1992.

———. *On the Phenomenology of the Consciousness of Internal Time.* Trans. John Barnett Brough. Dordrecht: Kluwer, 1991.

Jay, Martin. *Downcast Eyes. The Denigration of Vision in Twentieth-Century French Thought.* Berkeley: University of California Press, 1993.

Kafka, Franz. *The Diaries of Franz Kafka.* Trans. Joseph Kresh and Martin Greenberg (with Hannah Arendt). New York: Schocken, 1964.

Klee, Paul. *On Modern Art.* Trans. Paul Findlay. London: Faber, 1966. Translation of *Théorie de l'art moderne.* 1956. Paris: Essais, 1998.

Kracauer, Siegfried. *From Caligari to Hitler.* Princeton, NJ: Princeton University Press, 1947.

Kuhn, Thomas S. *The Structure of Scientific Revolutions.* 1961. Chicago: University of Chicago Press, 1996.

La politique des auteurs: Entretiens avec J. Renoir, R. Rossellini, F. Lang, et al. Preface by Serge Daney. Paris: Cahiers du cinéma, 2001.

Laugier, Sandra, and Marc Cerisuelo, eds. *Stanley Cavell: Cinéma et philosophie.* Paris: Presses de la Sorbonne Nouvelle, 2001.

Levinas, Emmanuel. *Existence and Existents.* Trans. Alphonso Lingis. Pittsburgh: Duquesne University Press, 1978. Translation of *De l'existence à l'existant.* 1947. Paris: Vrin, 1986.

Marrati, Paola. "Against the Doxa: Politics of Immanence and Becoming-Minoritarian." In Pisters, *Micropolitics of Media Culture,* 205–20.

———. "L'animal qui sait fuir. G. Deleuze: Politique du devenir, ontologie de l'immanence." In *L'animal autobiographique,* ed. Marie-Louise Mallet, 197–214. Paris: Galilée, 1999.

———. "Contro la doxa: Filosofia e letteratura nell'opera di G. Deleuze." In *Il potere delle parole,* ed. Silvano Petrosino, 145–70. Rome: Bulzoni, 2000.

Merleau-Ponty, Maurice. *Sens et non-sens.* 1966. Paris: Gallimard, 1996.

Metz, Christian. *Film Language: A Semiotics of the Cinema.* Trans. Michael Taylor. New York: Oxford University Press, 1974. Translation of *Essais sur la signification au cinéma.* Vol. 1. 1968. Paris: Klincksieck, 1983.

Mitry, Jean. *The Aesthetics and Psychology of the Cinema.* Trans. Christopher King. Bloomington: Indiana University Press, 1997. Translation of *Esthétique et psychologie du cinéma.* Paris: Éditions universitaires, 1965.

———. *Histoire du cinéma muet.* Vol. 3, *1923–1930.* Paris: Éditions Universitaires, 1973.

Nietzsche, Friedrich. *Untimely Meditations.* Ed. Daniel Breazeal. Trans. R. J. Hollingdale. Cambridge, UK: Cambridge University Press, 1997.

Pasolini, Pier Paolo. *Heretical Empiricism.* Trans. Ben Lawton and Louise K. Barnett. Bloomington: Indiana University Press, 1988.

Patton, Paul. *Deleuze and the Political.* London: Routledge, 2002.

———. "Redescriptive Philosophy: Deleuze and Guattari's Critical Pragmatism." In Pisters, *Micropolitics of Media Culture,* 29–42.

Pearson, Keith Ansell. *Philosophy and the Adventure of the Virtual: Bergson and the Time of Life.* London: Routledge, 2002.

Pisters, Patricia, ed. *Micropolitics of Media Culture.* Amsterdam: Amsterdam University Press, 2001.

Prigogine, Ilya, and Isabelle Stengers. *La nouvelle alliance.* Paris: Gallimard, 1986.

Prochiantz, Alain. "À propos d'Henri Bergson: Être et ne pas être un animal." *Critique,* no. 661–62 (June–July 2002): 542–51.

Proust, Marcel. *Time Regained.* Trans C. K. Scott Montcrieff, Terence Kilmartin, and Andreas Mayor. New York: Vintage, 1982.

Rancière, Jacques. *La fable cinématographique.* Paris: Le Seuil, 2001.

Robbe-Grillet, Alain. *For a New Novel.* Trans. Richard Howard. New York: Grove Press, 1965. Translation of *Pour un nouveau roman.* Paris: Minuit, 1961.

Rodowick, D. N. "La critique ou la vérité en crise." *Iris* 23 (spring 1997): 7–24.

———. *Gilles Deleuze's Time Machine.* Durham, NC: Duke University Press, 1997.

Rorty, Richard. *Philosophy and Social Hope.* London: Penguin, 1999.

Sartre, Jean-Paul. *L'imagination.* 1936. Paris: PUF, 2000.

Schefer, Jean-Louis. *L'homme ordinaire du cinéma.* Paris: Cahiers du cinéma, 1980.

Smith, Daniel. "The Place of Ethics in Deleuze's Philosophy: Three Questions of Immanence." In *Deleuze and Guattari,* ed. Eleanor Kaufman and Kevin Jon Heller, 251–69. Minneapolis: University of Minnesota Press, 1998.

Tarkovsky, Andrei. *Sculpting in Time: Reflections on the Cinema.* Trans. Kitty Hunter-Blair. Austin: University of Texas Press, 1989.

Vertov, Dziga. *Kino-Eye: The Writings of Dziga Vertov.* Ed. Annette Michelson. Trans. Kevin O'Brien. Berkeley: University of California Press, 1984.

Worms, Frédéric. *Introduction à "Matière et mémoire" de Bergson.* Paris: PUF, 1997.

Zourabichvili, François. *Deleuze: Une philosophie de l'événement.* Paris: PUF, 1994.

———. "Deleuze et le possible (de l'involontarisme en politique)." In *Gilles Deleuze. Une vie philosophique,* ed. Eric Alliez, 355–57. Paris: Les Empêcheurs de penser en ronde, 1998.

———. "The Eye of Montage: Dziga Vertov and Bergsonian Materialism." In *The Brain Is the Screen: Deleuze and the Philosophy of Cinema,* ed. Gregory Flaxman, 141–52. Minneapolis: University of Minnesota Press, 2000.

Index

Achilles and the tortoise, 11–12
action, x, xii–xv, 30, 55, 63; and perception, 10, 33–34, 36, 49, 59–60,
72. *See also* agency
action film, 48, 61
action-form, x, 4, 101, 103–4; crisis
of the, 5
action-images, x, xii, 35, 38, 51; crisis
of, 55, 61–63, 65, 79, 81, 85, 104–5
Actor's Studio, the, 117n5
actual, 11, 71–74; in Foucault, 122n13
Adventure, The (Antonioni), 107
affect, 41–42, 52, 100
affection-images, x, 35, 38, 41–42, 60
agency, x, xiii–xv, 101. *See also* action
American cinema, 45, 47–48, 51,
53–55, 79, 104. *See also* Hollywood
American dream, 53–54, 62, 102
ancient philosophy and science,
13–14, 16. *See also* Aristotle; Plato
and Platonism; Zeno
Anti-Oedipus (Deleuze and Guattari), x
Antonioni, Michelangelo, 21, 60,
61, 62, 77, 87, 107, 109
any-instant-whatever, 8, 13, 14
any-point-whatever, 23, 61, 118n11
Aristotle, xii, 10, 15, 90

Balibar, Etienne, 124n26
Barabas, Renaud, 115n14
Battleship Potemkin (Eisenstein),
50, 51

Bazin, André, 25, 98, 100; and
Deleuze, 1, 76, 86, 119n3, 122n21;
and neorealism, 39, 56–69, 107–8
becoming, 10, 17, 64, 84–85
behavior, 52, 100–101
being, 89–90
belief, 5, 85–86, 87–88, 104, 106,
108–9
Bellour, Raymond, 125n33
Benjamin, Walter, 81
Bensmaïa, Réda, 118n11
Bergson, Henri, 7–43, 68–77; and
the actual, 73–74; and cinema,
3–4, 9–16, 26, 28, 32, 37, 68,
76; and consciousness, 3, 29–33,
35–36; and Einstein, 30; and images, 28–36; and Kant, 113n9,
115n15; and movement, 8–19; and
perception 3, 27, 33–36, 69–70,
115n13; and phenomenology, 29,
36; as philosopher of immanence,
5, 92; and time, 14–16, 68–77;
and the universe, 3, 19, 32, 37, 40,
42, 91–93; and the virtual, 73–74
Bergson, Henri, works: *Creative
Mind*, 36, 49; *Duration and Simultaneity*, 31, 115n10; *Time and
Free Will: An Essay on the Immediate Data of Consciousness*, 17.
See also *Creative Evolution;* living
images; *Matter and Memory*
Birth of a Nation, The (Griffith), 46,
98–99

133

Index

blocs of space-time, 19, 30–31, 39, 42
Bonitzer, Pascal, 22
Bresson, Robert, 88, 97, 123n23
Burch, Noël, 52, 114n15

Capra, Frank, 117n7
Casetti, Francesco, 117n2, 122n19
Catholicism of cinema, 80–81, 85
Cavell, Stanley, 6, 98, 110–11, 115n5,
    122–23n21; *This New Yet Unap-
    proachable America*, 110; *The
    World Viewed*, 98, 122–23n21
center of indetermination, 33–34, 42
Cerisuelo, Marc. *See* Laugier,
    Sandra, and Marc Cerisuelo
Chaplin, Charlie, 121n3
cine-eye, 37
cinema of the seer, xiii, 58–59, 85, 107
cinematographic illusion, 9, 13,
    15–16, 86, 104
Citizen Kane (Welles), 68, 76–77,
    119n3
classic and modern cinema, 4, 63,
    68, 79, 104, 116n32
classic cinema, x, 51, 63, 79
close-up, 24, 41, 46
community, 53, 101–2, 105, 117n7
concepts, 7, 18, 48–49, 91, 94–95
consciousness, 28–36, 52
creation, 14, 16, 41, 45, 50, 95, 122n12
Creative Evolution (Bergson), 9–17,
    19, 22–23
crystal or crystalline images, 68,
    72–74

Daney, Serge, 121n7
deframing [*décadrage*], 22, 37
depth (of field), 20, 57–58, 76
Derrida, Jacques, 121n4
Descartes, René, 8
De Sica, Vittorio, 107
Difference and Repetition (Deleuze),
    79, 82–83, 89–92

Dreyer, Carl, 22, 23, 51, 87
duel, 46, 49, 53, 101
Duns Scotus, Johannes, 90
duration, 12, 17, 25, 39, 44–45, 59, 76
    Duration and Simultaneity (Berg-
    son), 31, 115n10

Eclipse, The (Antonioni), 107
Einstein, Albert, 19, 30–31, 115n10
Eisenstein, Sergei: critique of Grif-
    fith, xi, 49, 99–100, 103; and
    montage, 44, 49–51, 63, 66; vio-
    lence or shock of images in, 79,
    80, 85, 105, 106
Emerson, Ralph Waldo, 110–11
Epstein, Jean, 42, 67, 116n29, 118n2
eternal return, 84
Europe 51 (Rossellini), 58–59, 107
event, 64, 122n15
experience, 7, 36–37
expression, 41, 116n30

faith, 63, 85–89, 108
Fascism, 55, 81
Faure, Elie, 80, 121n4
Fellini, Federico, 60, 107
Fichte, Johann Gottlieb, 88
film noir, 53, 101
Fitzgerald, F. Scott, 53, 117n6
Ford, John, 97, 109
Foucault, Michel, 122n13
frame or framing, 20–24, 33, 62.
    See also deframing; freeze-frame;
    out-of-field
freeze-frame, 93
French New Wave. See *nouvelle
    vague*
Freud, Sigmund, 123n25
future, 15, 16, 68, 73, 84

Galileo, 8, 14
Germany Year Zero (Rossellini),
    56–58, 107

Index

Marrati, Paola, 116n27, 124n26, 124n28
Marxist philosophy, xi, xii, 110
Matter and Memory (Bergson), 3, 4, 19, 27–34, 68–77, 91–92
Mendeleyev, Dmitri, 43
Merleau-Ponty, Maurice, 36, 52, 115n14, 117n5
Metz, Christian, 1, 48,
milieu, 52, 79, 100–101
Minnelli, Vincente, 97
Mitry, Jean, 38, 114n15, 116n20
mobile section. *See* sections
modern cinema, x, 39, 56–65, 79, 81, 85–87, 111. *See also* neorealism
modernity, 3, 27–28, 42, 87–89, 109, 111
modern science, 8–9, 13–14, 16, 18
montage, 44–55; Bazin on, 57; the close-up in, 46, 98; concurrent or convergent, 46, 49, 98; as direct image of time, 45; in Eisenstein, x, 49–51, 66, 99–100; in Griffith, 46–48, 49, 51, 98–99; and history, 104; as indirect image of time, 39, 44–51, 54, 66; modern, 119n4; in neorealism, 57; of opposition, 50, 100; organico-active, x, 45, 47, 48, 54–55, 99; organico-dialectic, x, 45, 50, 99–100; organic unity and, 46–47, 50, 98–99; parallel alternate, 45, 49, 98; in Pasolini, 66; in Vertov, 37–38
Moral Tales (Rohmer), 88
movement, 6–26; aberrant or abnormal, 67–68, 118n2; absolute, 91
movement-images, 2, 20–26, 104; and montage, 44–45, 48–51, 54–55; temporality of, 66–67; universe of, 3–4, 19–20, 29–32, 35, 37, 40, 71–72; varieties of, 38

Narration, 48, 49, 98, 99, 100
narrative cinema, 33, 48
Nazism, 55, 56. *See also* Hitler and Hitlerism
neorealism, 4, 39, 56–59, 85, 107
Nietzsche, Friedrich, 83, 88, 90, 106–7, 109, 122n13; and history, 54, 64, 102–3, 105
Nietzsche and Philosophy (Deleuze), 4, 84
nouveau roman, 70–71, 118n12
nouvelle vague, 4, 71

October (Eisenstein), 51
ontology: of cinema, 98; of images, 4, 27–28, 40; of immanence, 89–90; of time, 72–77
Open, the, 17–18, 44–45, 91
organism, xi, 49–51, 46, 99–100
out-of-field, 22–24
Ozu, Yasujiro, 21, 62, 77, 97, 118n9

Panofsky, Erwin, 122n21
Pascal, Blaise, 87, 109
Pasolini, Pier Paolo, 39, 44, 66, 87, 118n13
Passion of Joan of Arc, The (Dreyer), 22, 23, 51
past, 15, 68, 73–77
Patton, Paul, 123n22, 124n26
Pearson, Keith Ansell, 120n9
Peirce, Charles Saunders, 21, 116n31
people, 79, 123–24n26
perception, 27–43; attentive, 69–70; automatic or habitual, 59, 69; cinematographic or photographic, 9–11, 25, 27; pragmatic, 39, 60, 64, 116n22; pure, 107–8; and recognition, 59–60, 107; sensorimotor, 34, 36, 39, 60; and time, 67–68. *See also* perception-images; *and under* action; Bergson

Index

time *(continued)*
ontological nature of, 72–77;
pure, 78; and truth, 83. *See also*
future; past; present; time-
images; *and under* Bergson
*Time and Free Will: An Essay on the
Immediate Data of Consciousness*
(Bergson), 17
time-images, 2, 20, 66–77, 78; direct, 39–40, 45, 59, 67; indirect,
39, 45–55, 67
transcendence, 63, 81, 93, 110
truth, 83–84

Untimely Meditations (Nietzsche),
54, 102

Vernant, Jean-Pierre, 90
Vertov, Dziga, 37–38, 51, 79, 97,
116nn18–19
Vidor, King, 101

virtual images, 71–74, 120n9
Visconti, Luchino, 60, 107

Welles, Orson, 20, 57, 68, 76–77,
97, 119n3
What Is Cinema? (Bazin), 25. *See
also* Bazin, André
What Is Philosophy? (Deleuze and
Guattari), 4–5, 89–93, 95–96
Whole, the, 17–18, 23, 25, 39; mon-
tage and, 44–45, 47–48, 50–51, 54
world, 79–80, 85, 87, 88–89, 104–11,
122n20
world-becoming, 121n4
World War II, x, 55, 61–63, 111
Worms, Frédéric, 115n6
Wyler, William, 20, 97

Zeno, 11, 16
Zourabichivili, François, 116n18,
124n26

138